Instant Self-Hypnosis

How to
Hypnotize Yourself
with
Your Eyes Open

FORBES ROBBINS BLAIR

SOURCEBOOKS, INC.®
NAPERVILLE, ILLINOIS

Published by Sourcebooks, Inc.
P.O. Box 4410, Naperville, Illinois 60567-4410
(630) 961-3900
FAX: (630) 961-2168
www.sourcebooks.com

Library of Congress Cataloging-in-Publication Data

Blair, Forbes Robbins.
  Instant self-hypnosis : how to hypnotize yourself with your eyes open / Forbes Robbins Blair.
    p. cm.
  ISBN 1-4022-0269-5 (alk. paper)
  1. Autogenic training. I. Title.
  RC499.A8B56 2004
  615.8'5122—dc22
                                                                    2003027757

States of America
14 13

Acknowledgments

Grateful acknowledgement is made to the following people and organizations:

Deb Werksman, editor, and the staff of Sourcebooks—for the vision to take on this project. Carole Abel, literary agent—for helping me navigate unfamiliar territory. Deb Leopold, President of First Class, Inc.—for allowing me to teach and refine the techniques of Instant Self-Hypnosis. Robert Morrison, best friend—for his constant assistance, technical expertise, and support. Luann Fulbright, friend and fellow seeker, for her help and enthusiasm. Dr. Christopher Morrison and the American Institute of Hypnotherapy—for introducing hypnotherapy to me and changing the course of my professional life. Kristin Blair Cooper, sister and attorney—for her legal counsel and her manifestation abilities. My mother, Hilma R. Blair, who encouraged my interest in hypnosis when I was a boy by taking me to the library so I could learn more about it.

Table of Contents

Preface

If you are like many people, you've heard how hypnosis has helped others achieve their goals. You've even thought about different ways you might use hypnosis to change your own life for the better.

Maybe you'd like to be hypnotized to improve your physical body to get lean and trim, stay motivated to exercise, or to stop smoking once and for all.

Or maybe you're feeling stress in your life. You'd like to be hypnotized to let go of that tension and to feel more relaxed? Who wouldn't?

Perhaps you'd improve your mental abilities through hypnosis. Have you imagined how your life might change if you possessed Zen-like focus and concentration? Have you wished for a sharper memory? To ace that test coming up? Or maybe just to remember the names of people you meet?

Perhaps you've wondered if hypnosis could help you be more loving toward your mate or to spruce up your sex life?

So Why Aren't You Going to a Professional Hypnotist?

Again, if you are like many people, thinking about ways hypnotherapy might help you is as far as you've gone. Or you've gone once or twice to a hypnotist but you just didn't continue. The reasons people don't go to a hypnotist are often these:

- You don't have the time to go to the hypnotist's office.
- You don't have—or don't want—to spend the money.

• You're too timid. Is hypnosis safe? Are your issues just too
  personal to discuss with a hypnotist...or anyone?

Now You Don't Need to Go to a Professional

The good news is, now that you have this book, you don't need to go
to a professional hypnotist. Just sit right there and read! Instant Self-
Hypnosis enables you to hypnotize yourself to accomplish virtually
any goals without ever putting down the book. The book does the
work for you!

Even more startling, you will learn to hypnotize yourself with your
eyes open! Unlike other forms of hypnosis, with Instant Self-Hypnosis
there's no reason to close your eyes throughout the entire procedure.

The best part of all is that the can't-fail methods of Instant Self-
Hypnosis are so easy to use. You'll succeed the very first time you try
them. The procedures are so efficient, applying them to a goal takes
as little as fifteen minutes.

Please do not confuse Instant Self-Hypnosis with any other books
or audio programs about hypnosis or self-hypnosis. It's unlike anything you've read, heard about, or tried. It's a revolutionary book
offering you an extraordinary technique with distinct advantages over
traditional methods of self-help hypnosis. This user-friendly book can
change your life in practical ways, and you'll be able to put it to work
for you in just minutes...if you keep reading.

Get ready to learn about an innovative discovery in self-
improvement—Instant Self-Hypnosis.

Introduction
A Breakthrough in Self-Help

This book is about a breakthrough discovery in hypnosis and self-improvement. In 1997 I discovered an unusual method for inducing hypnosis. As a professional hypnotherapist, I've been teaching, testing, and refining it ever since. I call the technique Instant Self-Hypnosis. It involves the reading and writing of hypnosis scripts as a means of entering a state of hypnosis. This method of hypnosis may be used for a wide range of therapeutic purposes: removing bad habits, confidence building, goal attainment, and so much more. This can't-fail technique requires no experience or knowledge of hypnosis whatsoever. Plus, it's so simple that you may marvel that no one previously thought of it…or if they did think of it, why they never published the discovery. Or if they did publish it, how come no one knows about it?

Instant Self-Hypnosis is ingenious in its efficacy and simplicity. I call Instant Self-Hypnosis a discovery rather than an invention because the method has been "hidden in plain sight" perhaps for as long as hypnotherapy has been in existence. What I've done is recognize its potential value and develop it in such a way any intelligent person can put to good use.

Why is *Instant Self-Hypnosis* not your average self-improvement book? This publication does something that most self-help books cannot do. Most self-help authors give advice or enumerate steps to be followed after you've read their books. That is, only when you put those books down can you begin to put their advice into practice. But with *Instant Self-Hypnosis,* there is no delay.

You benefit fully from this book without ever putting it aside. It's designed to change you as you read it! With this innovation in self-improvement, there are no words of wisdom to remember. There are no skills to practice. There are no traits or steps of "highly perfect people" to emulate! This book and its techniques are self-contained. The help is immediate. The results materialize automatically.

This book is for anyone who wants—or needs—a potent, valuable tool for positive personal change. If you are new to hypnosis or self-help media, Instant Self-Hypnosis gives you a fast and easy means for improving the quality of your life in many areas. If you are an avid consumer of do-it-yourself material, you will find Instant Self-Hypnosis a friendly alternative to some of the other techniques you might have tried. If you are a professional hypnotherapist or a psychologist, you will be intrigued by the powerful simplicity of Instant Self-Hypnosis. Its operative principles have many implications and applications for the fields of hypnotherapy, psychology, and psychoimmunology.

The Things You Will Learn

The heart of this book revolves around the hands-on learning of Instant Self-Hypnosis. The book takes you through a fun exercise that not only introduces you to the concepts of Instant Self-Hypnosis but actually hypnotizes you as you perform it! The exercise acts as a proactive primer to ensure success with all subsequent endeavors with Instant Self-Hypnosis. After that, you'll apply the method to your goals, using the appropriate scripts.

As mentioned, you don't have to know a thing about hypnosis to put Instant Self-Hypnosis to work for you. But some basic knowledge is certainly a good thing to possess in any endeavor you undertake. Part One of the book tells you what you need to know about the power of your subconscious mind and how it relates to hypnosis. You'll also learn about these things:

- what hypnosis and self-hypnosis are and whether you are hypnotizable;
- the misconceptions and ill-founded fears some people have about hypnosis and how safe it truly is;
- how hypnosis and traditional self-hypnosis work and the problems associated with conventional methods;
- my discovery: what it is, how it works, and how it automatically avoids the troubling pitfalls associated with traditional techniques; and
- a powerful hypnotic primer, which lets you experience its power and simplicity firsthand!

In Part Two, you'll be shown how to put the technique to work for thirty-five common hypnosis goals, using professionally prepared hypnosis scripts. In Part Three, you'll learn another aspect of Instant Self-Hypnosis that shows you how to customize the technique for virtually any self-improvement goal, no matter how unique it may be. I have taught this customization process for several years in a course called "How to Hypnotize Yourself with Your Eyes Open," and students have found it easy to master.

The book wraps up with some important tips to ensure success with Instant Self-Hypnosis. Additionally, it clarifies answers to some frequently asked questions regarding the techniques and their proper application. And don't forget to check out the Bonus sections toward the end of the book. For instance, you may want to take the Instant Self-Hypnosis Stress-Buster Challenge.

This publication is written in a conversational style. I have tried neither to wow you with flowery prose nor impress you with the sometimes excessive jargon of my profession. I also refuse to waste your time telling you about "Case study #73: How Ethel Jones benefited from my method." What a snooze! If you're anything like me, you want to get to the good stuff as fast as possible. So I'll tell you only what you really need to now to put Instant Self-Hypnosis directly to work for you—as soon as possible.

When you apply Instant Self-Hypnosis techniques to your desires and see the way your life improves quickly and easily, you won't need hyped-up anecdotes to convince you of its power. You will know because of your success—the wonderful tool you now have at your fingertips.

Part One

1

It's All in Your Mind

This chapter reviews the function and relationship between the conscious and subconscious aspects of the mind. I'll also discuss why changing your thoughts and behaviors, even with a good plan, can be challenging. And you'll discover why hypnosis is such an effective tool for promoting self-change.

Two Minds in One

Have you wondered why it can be so difficult to change your unwanted behaviors or attitudes? For instance, why can't you just decide with one emphatic decision to stop smoking, to put the donuts aside, or to just relax more and have a more enjoyable life experience? Here is a quick explanation. Part of you says, "Yes, I will change." Another part of you is saying, "No way. I'm not changing!" It's almost like there are two minds inhabiting each of us, disagreeing on what should change and what shouldn't.

Obviously your mind is very complex. In fact, you should make a beeline away from anyone who claims to totally understand it. But there are some things about the mind that seem evident.

You have one mind with (at least) two different aspects. We'll refer to these as your conscious mind and your subconscious mind. The conscious mind, also called the objective mind, includes your current field of awareness. It's the part of you that has decided to read this book right now. It's the part of you that makes the decisions, like what you eat for breakfast, whom to call on the telephone, or where to go after work. Your subconscious is the part of your mind that functions below the surface of your awareness. It's the part of you that is deciphering the symbols on this page right now—symbols you painstakingly learned when you were younger, which you now automatically recognize as words.

Your subconscious mind also runs the functions of your body. It knows exactly how fast to make your heart beat, how to digest your breakfast, and a lot of other tasks about which you've probably never given much conscious thought. Some of the tasks it knows how to do are built in from birth, like your bodily functions. Other tasks, like reading, are taught to it through the conscious mind. The subconscious has access to all of your memories. It holds all of your values and beliefs intact and efficiently recalls frequently used behavior patterns.

The conscious mind and the subconscious mind communicate with each other whether you are aware of it or not. The conscious mind, for instance, sends messages to the subconscious mind that you want to use your arm and hand muscles to turn the page of a book. Since it has long learned the exact muscles, movements, and coordination required for the task, it complies easily and quickly. The subconscious doesn't work against the conscious mind, but sometimes it can appear that way, for the subconscious is resistant to sudden change. This is especially true when you attempt to change a longstanding behavior, belief, or attitude...mainly because of your "programming."

Programs of the Mind

There's an old saying among computer programmers—"Garbage in, garbage out." It means that if you put bad data into a computer, you can expect the output to be less than great.

The mind is like a very complex computer in some ways. Your thought patterns and behavioral sequences are like installed programs in a computer. Some of them were installed by you. For example, maybe the first time you ever ate chocolate, you enjoyed the taste and texture and you began to eat it often, and to this day you have formed a pattern of eating chocolate on a regular basis. Other programs were installed by your parents or teachers. For instance, they might have encouraged or exposed you to classical and neoclassical art, and now as an adult you deeply appreciate and collect classic artwork.

Likewise, your peers (from childhood on) may have contributed to your mental programming. Let's say your friends invited you to smoke a cigarette. It was uncomfortable and hardly pleasurable for you—at first. Then you began to associate a feeling of relaxation and acceptance with it. Thirty years later, you're still smoking and subconsciously associating that activity with feelings of relaxation because that program was etched in your mind and becomes activated whenever you feel stressed. Just as the programs of a computer may be activated with the right commands, the programs of your mind are ready and waiting in your subconscious mind to activate whenever a certain sequence of thoughts, words, or events take place. This is the very essence of learning and usually works to your advantage. Sometimes, however, you come to the realization that you no longer want or need a certain set of thoughts or behaviors. Maybe you want to get rid of some garbage that you put in your mind long ago. Perhaps you simply want to add a program, a new attitude or behavior that appeals to you. You desire to change the programming.

Change the Programming

Changing, installing, or uninstalling a computer program is a relatively easy task. But it isn't so easy to alter the programs of your mind. And that's actually a good thing.

Your mind comes complete with a filter, a protector that acts like a built-in security system. This filter screens new thoughts and behaviors, making sure you really want what you say you want. It weighs new ideas and information against current knowledge and beliefs. It's very slow to accept sudden changes that are inconsistent with the old programs, the old way of thinking and doing things.

This works to your benefit to keep your beliefs, personality, and your sense of reality consistent, for your subconscious mind is, in and of itself, nondiscriminatory. Any idea or suggestion allowed past the mental filter is accepted as true. So the security system keeps you from changing your mind constantly and from accepting every suggestion that comes your way. If it didn't, you'd end up in a state of confusion. Imagine, for instance, what kind of chaos would result if your mind didn't screen the hundreds of advertisements you see every day. But this can certainly be troublesome when you want to alter something in your life. The security system of the mind can often reject ideas for change that you intend for your own good, even suggestions coming from your own conscious thoughts. It can prevent those good ideas from becoming a part of your inner programming, from becoming a part of your daily life. It does this because it bases its evaluation of all new ideas, even good ones, on previously accepted beliefs and interpretations of experience. For instance, a lot of smokers have a difficult time quitting because they have accepted a belief that it is hard to stop smoking. This belief sabotages their effort and will power.

There are several ways to deal with the security system of the mind, but some are more expedient than others. Some people, for instance, by sheer force of will, repeat a new behavior until it becomes automatic. This method is often beset with setbacks and frustrations. But with perseverance, these iron-willed souls sometimes succeed in changing themselves because performing an activity over and over can override the mind's security system. The inner mind eventually accepts the new way of doing things, and it forms a new habit pattern.

Another way to handle the mind's security system is by using affirmations. Through repetition of positive statements, it's possible to make desired changes. Over a period of days, weeks, or months, the mind gets to a point of saturation. It gradually begins to accept the affirmations as true, bringing about the intended outcome. Results are often slow in coming, however, often leading to doubt and frustration.

Many people neither possess the iron-willed resolve to strong-arm their minds into accepting a new set of beliefs and behaviors nor the patience and faith needed to effectively apply daily affirmations.

Fortunately, there is an easier method for dealing with the security system of the mind.

Disarming the Mind's Security System with Hypnosis

Hypnosis offers an expedient method for that change. It disarms or bypasses the security system of the mind just long enough to communicate directly with the inner mind. And with the security system in a stand-by mode, the mind instantly begins accepting suggestions at face value—whether it's to stop smoking, to stay faithful to your new diet, or any other concept you want your inner mind to absorb. Your suggestions are like a new program, and hypnosis allows you to install the program without the usual interference of doubts and questions that bombard the mind. This makes change faster and easier than the aforementioned methods. This is what makes hypnosis such a powerful and preferable tool for change.

Getting Past the Doorman (a.k.a. the Bouncer)

For those of you who can't relate to a computer analogy, an exclusive nightclub offers another way to understand hypnosis and the security system of the mind. If you've ever tried to get into a popular nightclub, the kind where only certain types of people are let in and others are kept out, you may have had to deal with the doorman (a.k.a. the bouncer) who makes these decisions. Usually the doorman is big, muscular, and intimidating. You might say that your mind has its own doorman—a gatekeeper, so to speak. The nightclub is like your subconscious—the place where everything is happening, the place you want to get into. And what happens when you approach a strong doorman to get inside the club is very similar to what happens when you attempt to change some longstanding behavior or attitude. The doorman looks you over to determine whether he thinks you are someone who belongs in the club. He bases his decision on what kind of people are already inside, what kind of club it is, and what the management has told him. In a similar manner, when a new idea for change or improvement comes up to the doorman of your inner mind, the idea is weighed to decide if it "fits in" to previously established ideas and behaviors. If it doesn't meet that criteria, the idea is rejected; the doorman turns you away.

There are several ways to deal with a doorman. You can try to fight him to get into the club. But unless you're bigger and stronger, this is likely to get you into the emergency room instead. This method is used by those people I mentioned who strong-arm their minds into accepting a new behavior. Again, it can be done, but it is a daunting task...and you might get a bit banged up even if you succeed. Another way to deal with the doorman is to stay at the door hour after hour nagging him to let you into the club. This is akin to using affirmations to get your inner mind to change. If you do it enough, you might succeed eventually—but there's no guarantee of that, of course. There might be another way to deal with the doorman, though. What if you could get a pretty woman to talk to him in a low, sultry voice and distract his attention away from the door just long enough for you to slip by him? Yeah, that would work. And this very similar to what hypnosis does. It calms, quiets, and distracts the doorman of your mind so that you can get inside, make some changes, then leave again. With hypnosis, there's no need to strong-arm or annoy the gatekeeper. Instead, the process is smooth and calming. And the great thing is that this trick works every time. The doorman can always be sweet-talked and lulled to distraction. In fact, the doorman may enjoy the experience so much that he looks forward to it in the future. Likewise, hypnosis is so pleasant it becomes easier and easier every time. It is something your mind enjoys and looks forward to.

It's All in Your Mind—Summary

- The subconscious aspect of your mind is very important to your life, your memories, and your behaviors.
- It can be difficult to access the subconscious mind to make beneficial changes because of your mind's security system.
- Hypnosis allows you to bypass that system and instruct the subconscious mind about the changes you would like to make in your body, your mind, and your behavior.

2

What You Should Know about Hypnosis

In this chapter, we'll discover where the word *hypnosis* came from and why we will use hypnosis for personal improvement for a long time to come regardless of what name it's given. We'll explore what hypnosis isn't as well as what it is. Plus, you'll find out whether you can be hypnotized. We'll examine how traditional hypnosis and self-hypnosis are induced and what problems are associated with conventional methods.

"Scooby-Doo" Hypnosis

People have a lot of strange or exaggerated notions about what hypnosis is, how it is applied, and what happens when you are hypnotized. My first exposure to hypnosis occurred when I was boy as I watched a first-run episode of the cartoon *Scooby-Doo, Where Are You?* There was a particular episode in which an evil haunted-circus clown went around with a shiny gold pocket watch, hypnotizing the Scooby gang into unwillingly doing all sorts of bizarre and dangerous things. The clown swung the watch in front of Scooby, whose eyes grew wide as he became spellbound by some unexplainable force. Once the Great Dane was hypnotized, the clown made Scooby walk a tightrope while in a deep trance. And as long as Scooby stayed in the magical trance, he was able to do it with perfect ease. This totally fascinated me. Right after the cartoon I asked my mother if I could learn about hypnosis. She called libraries all over town. There was a small one not too far away that had one book on the subject. We hopped in the car and headed to that library, where a bemused librarian checked out a blue paperback book on hypnosis to a precocious boy.

I got the book home and started reading immediately. I quickly skipped the front material (which I still do with most self-help books), the parts telling me the "where and why" of hypnosis, and went right for the "how to" chapter. As I read, it seemed easy enough, so I talked one of my closest buddies into letting me experiment with him as the hypnotic subject. We went down to my parents' basement and I sat him in a comfortable chair as the book told me to do. It also said to put a bright light in front of him, just above eye level, and to have him gaze into it. Being a child, I tended to understand things literally, so I put the bright light only about a foot away from his face and had him look into it. It's a wonder he didn't go blind, in retrospect. Anyway, I sat just behind and to his right and followed the instructions, attempting to lull him into a hypnotic trance. I watched and waited expectantly to observe a zombielike glaze in my friend's eyes like I saw in the cartoon. Minutes went by and by and by. The only thing that happened is that my friend's eyes started to tear up because I told him not to blink as he stared into the bright light. As for the signs of trance? Nothing. Didn't happen. How disappointing! Back to the drawing board. So I read the book again and again, and I tried several times to hypnotize my friend in the days that followed. But nothing even remotely similar to what I saw on *Scooby-Doo* happened to my friend, so I finally put hypnosis on the back burner and wouldn't come back to it for another fourteen years.

I tell you this story because it illustrates the silly misconceptions that a person may have about hypnosis, often based on works of fiction. These notions can create unrealistic and even undesirable expectations, leading you away from a rational, sane approach to the subject. It is the job of the trained hypnotherapists to reeducate clients and the public about hypnosis, the kind used for therapeutic ends.

The Half-Truths of Stage Hypnosis

Stage hypnotists are often also the source of spreading misinformation about hypnosis. I remember going to see a stage hypnotist act when I was in college. From the audience's point of view, it looked like he had entranced a dozen people on stage—that he could make them say or do just about anything he commanded. One woman was told she was an alien and that she couldn't speak English. Sure enough, she tried to communicate to the audience with a language no one had ever heard before. He made the entire group think they were five years old, and they were asked what their favorite TV shows were. It was kind of funny when one of them said *Scooby-Doo.* It reminded me of my experiments with hypnosis ten years earlier. The show was funny; I don't think I've ever laughed so hard in my life. Boy, the joke sure was on those hypnotized people, wasn't it? Or was the joke on the audience who watched and believed that those on stage were deeply entranced and oblivious to the antics they performed?

It wasn't until years later when I began my certification course for clinical hypnotherapy that I began to understand what happens during stage hypnosis. As part of our training with the American Institute of Hypnotherapy, Dr. Christopher Wayne Morrison asked who would like to participate in a stage-type hypnosis experience. I raised my hand and went to the front of the class with about five other individuals. He had us close our eyes as he led us through a hypnotic induction. What I expected was what I saw on stage in college: to go into a deep trance in which I couldn't think for myself and which would cause me to lapse into unconsciousness as the hypnotist took over my mind and actions. That didn't happen. What did happen is that I felt very relaxed. I felt ready for something: expectant, willing, cooperative. So when Dr. Morrison told me that he was going to awaken me in a moment and that I would not remember the number *six,* I felt happy to oblige and to let those in the audience have a laugh seemingly at my expense but really at theirs. Sure enough, when he awakened me and asked me to count to ten, I counted out loud, "One, two, three, four, five, seven, eight, nine, ten." Sure enough, I omitted the number six in my count. Everybody laughed—except me. I felt like I was a good actor staying in character amidst audience reactions to a comedic play. There were other antics we were asked to do while in front of everyone. None of them were harmful or deeply embarrassing—just silly.

After the experience, Dr. Morrison asked the participants if that was what we expected. The answer was "no" from each of us. He went on to explain how stage hypnotists make it look as though the minds of participants are being controlled by the hypnotist, but that is just for show—an illusion. The reality is that people volunteer to participate in hypnosis and that they are in full control at all times. They do what is suggested to them by the hypnotist because they want to cooperate, for they have a part of them that is extroverted. (This surprised me, by the way, as I've always considered myself an introvert.) And the idea that you become a tranced-out zombie is really just fiction. At the same time, those who go on stage to be hypnotized actually do enter hypnosis! They enter into a state in which it becomes easy to cooperate, easy to tap the imaginative faculties and to express them if called upon to do so.

My experience verified this truth. While in front of the audience, it was very easy to get my full emotions into the tasks he suggested to me. I felt in no way inhibited or self-conscious—and that's unusual for most people when in front of a large group. So I could see that something, though I couldn't yet define what, happened to me as I was hypnotized in front of a group. It just wasn't what I was expecting because the stage hypnotist from my college days did a good job of entertaining me by letting me believe that he controlled the minds and actions of his subjects. And after all, the reason I went to the show in the first place was to be entertained. He most certainly succeeded, even though he left me with absolutely ridiculous notions about hypnosis, not to mention a bit of intrepidity.

I suppose this is my major objection to stage hypnosis, for it takes a legitimate form of therapy and turns it into a carnival act. And for this reason many people have a hard time taking hypnosis seriously. It's the same sort of problem those who've tried to legitimize cannabis (marijuana) ran into. Since it's been misused as a party drug for so long, most people have had a hard time realizing its therapeutic benefits, despite the evidence. This is why I decline whenever I am invited to perform my hypnotic services for entertainment value. Does this make me a party pooper? Maybe. But my mission is to get people like you to recognize and utilize hypnosis as the marvelous tool it is, and I can't do that by hypnotizing people to act like "teapots, short and stout."

Mesmerism and Hypnosis: Two Different Phenomena

You may well wonder, as I did, where the idea of the tranced-out, glazed-eyed hypnosis originated. That is, you may wonder if *Scooby-Doo* and the exaggerations of the stage-hypnosis shows have any basis in reality. And after doing some research and experimentation, I think the answer is that they do! That is, I believe there is actually a realistic basis for the notion of hypnosis being a very spacey trance state in which bizarre phenomena become possible. And basically the problem is one of semantics, for it seems that people have confused hypnosis with a phenomenon known as *mesmerism*. The two phenomena can be interrelated, and that's where the confusion originates.

Mesmerism is a term that came from the theories and practices of a man named Anton Mesmer, who hypothesized that a magnetic force comes out of the eyes of all human beings and that, if channeled in certain ways, can be used to heal or control the minds and bodies of others. He had all sorts of experiments designed to demonstrate this theory. Many of them were really quite bizarre and are downright funny to read about. There are some hypnotists even today who subscribe to the theory and practice of hypnosis by mesmerism. To learn to hypnotize others, they will tell you to build up the power of your gaze and then stare at the point between the eyebrows (e.g. the third eye) of your subject and project your ideas and will power to transfer suggestions. Is there truth to the notion of a magnetic force coming from the eyes?

As a student of mysticism and metaphysics, I must confess that I believe there is something to it. With a little knowledge and experimentation, it was possible to prove to myself that forces not yet measurable by scientific method are produced by the body and can be controlled by the mind. So I don't think Mesmer's hypothesis was as wacky as many have come to believe. And because mesmerism has as its intention the induction of a trance in which subjects become very suggestible, the mesmeric state must also be considered a hypnotic one by definition. So it can be successfully argued that mesmerism produces a hypnotic state.

The confusion comes when you are led to believe that only mesmerism can produce hypnosis; that is not at all the whole picture. The truth is that one may enter a hypnotic state through a variety of other methods having nothing to do with any "force" coming from the eyes or hands of the hypnotist. I think it is safe to say that most modern hypnotherapists aren't familiar with the use of mesmerism as a hypnotic technique. In fact, most of them would scoff at the notion. Most hypnotherapists use only the cooperation of the subject, relaxation, and suggestion to accomplish the task of producing hypnosis. And this works quite well. In fact, the premise of this book is that you don't need another person to enter hypnosis at all. You can do it for yourself, by yourself.

Hypnosis: A Recognized Form of Therapy

Hypnosis has been around a long time. It's a phenomenon that has been used as a form of therapy. The term *hypnosis* was coined by a man named Dr. James Braid back in the nineteenth century. The field of clinical hypnotherapy has been developing ever since. In the late 1950s, the American Medical Association approved hypnosis instruction for inclusion in medical schools. And hypnosis is considered by clinicians to be a serious topic in the healing arts.

Hypnosis and self-hypnosis are safe and efficient tools for growth and self-change, applicable to virtually every area of life. As I'll discuss later in detail, nearly everyone can be hypnotized. Hypnosis can help people physically, mentally, emotionally, and spiritually, and it's easy to learn and utilize. No fancy equipment is required to apply it. So once the basic tenets and techniques are understood, self-hypnosis can become easily applied. Self-hypnosis, too, can be used for almost any therapeutic end and is a form of self-therapy that is free of cost. This is especially welcome in the face of the rising cost of health care. And unlike drug therapies, there are no negative side effects to hypnosis, making it safe and friendly. These virtues are sure to make hypnosis popular for a long time to come.

Misconceptions about Hypnosis

The field has its army of skeptics, casual and adamant, mostly because of media misinformation. Who can forget some of the versions of hypnosis made famous by stage entertainers, television, and movies? For some, the term *hypnosis* has negative connotations; therefore, euphemisms like *active meditation* and *creative visualization* have risen in its place. It's important, therefore, to understand what hypnosis is not. There are so many erroneous ideas about what hypnosis is—its qualities and purposes. These notions can generate, if uncorrected, fear or false expectations.

To illustrate this, one day after a television interview I had done, the producer of the show and I got into a conversation about hypnosis. She asked with a smirk, "If hypnosis can really get people to stop smoking or lose weight, why aren't all of you hypnotists millionaires?"

My first instinct was to take offense to the question. After all, she was, in essence, calling into question the validity of my choice of profession. It's an unfair question. One could just as well ask why all physicians don't live in mansions or why all runners don't win gold medals.

But rather than becoming defensive, I redirected her question to produce this answer: the primary reason is because many people are afraid of hypnosis and are, therefore, reluctant to see a hypnotist. Their fears, however, are based on misinformation.

Let's discuss the most common misconceptions about hypnosis and replace them with the truth.

Misconception 1: Hypnosis is mind control. The truth is that during hypnosis you are in full control at all times. You may choose to accept or reject any suggestion made to you. Hypnosis does not turn you into some sort of robot or automaton. The idea that you surrender your will to the hypnotist is nonsense. Actually, the participation of your will power is crucial for effective hypnosis.

Misconception 2: Hypnosis is sleep. The truth is that during hypnosis you are wide awake. When the eyes are closed during traditional hypnosis, the body is generally still, so it may look as though one is asleep. It is true that some subjects accidentally drift off to sleep during a session, but when they do, they are no longer absorbing the hypnotic suggestions and will benefit very little from the hypnosis. The idea that hypnosis is sleep is often perpetuated by the hypnotist using the words *sleep* or *sleepy* during the process—"You are getting very sleepy." When using such words the hypnotist is not attempting to put the subject to sleep but is suggesting to the subject the idea of deep relaxation, which precedes sleep.

Misconception 3: Hypnosis creates amnesia. The uninitiated have been led to believe that when they are brought out of hypnosis they won't remember what went on during the session. While this is a possible phenomenon, it is rare. Most people fully remember everything that was said to them during hypnosis. This idea is perpetuated by stage shows where some participants claim not to remember what they did while under hypnosis. These claims are almost always ego-protecting fibs. Most stage subjects just don't go deeply enough into hypnosis to account for posthypnotic amnesia. The stage hypnotist is counting on widespread misconceptions about hypnosis to engender feelings of amazement and wonder from the audience, all in the name of entertainment. And the participants perpetuate this lie by pretending not to remember their on-stage antics.

Misconception 4: Hypnosis is a supernatural practice. Hypnosis is not a product of the occult or the New Age movement. As mentioned, the American Medical Association has, for decades, recognized hypnosis as a therapeutic tool that can be used for a broad variety of applications. It is true that hypnosis has been utilized toward spiritual ends, but there is nothing particularly "spiritual" about hypnosis and certainly nothing spooky about it. The process of being hypnotized is a natural and relaxing experience.

So What Is Hypnosis?

If you ask one hundred hypnotherapists for a definition of *hypnosis*, you'll likely get more than one hundred answers. The truth is that there is no consensus about the definition of *hypnosis*. For instance, I take part in a world-wide forum of hypnotherapists, and we always find ourselves arguing about what hypnosis is and what it isn't. Many of the definitions that are offered tend to describe how hypnosis is induced rather than what it actually is.

I have synthesized a short and broad definition for the sake of instruction. This definition may or may not be original but captures the essence of the phenomenon:

**Hypnosis is a state of narrowed attention in
which suggestibility is greatly heightened.**

This state is achieved through a wide variety of methods and can be used to impress upon the inner mind (a.k.a. the subconscious) all sorts of suggestions to have temporary or lasting effects. It is important to recognize that hypnosis doesn't create changes in subjects but instead creates a condition highly conducive to change.

The therapeutic use of the state turns mere hypnosis into hypnotherapy. While in a state of heightened suggestibility, positive ideas, values, and images may be impressed upon the inner mind of subjects to elicit beneficial changes. Whereas the stage hypnotist's suggestions are intended to last only for the duration of the act, suggestions given by the clinical hypnotherapist are designed to have an enduring effect after the actual hypnosis takes place.

Actually, therapeutic suggestions given to the hypnotized subject usually take one of two forms. While some suggestions are the type that attempt to impart an immediate change in belief, attitude, or behavior, other suggestions attempt to elicit a delayed response from the subject, a response designed to take effect after the hypnosis session is completed. The latter kind is known as a posthypnotic suggestion. Both are valid forms of suggestion, and both are frequently used during hypnotherapy.

Who Can Be Hypnotized?

The most common question a hypnotist hears from potential clients is, "Can I be hypnotized?" The answer is almost always, "Yes." What's funny is that some people defiantly believe themselves to be too strong-minded to be hypnotizable. This is like a weightlifter purporting to be too muscular to lift a can of peas.

Hypnosis is, in fact, a lot like a muscle—a muscle of the mind. It's both a process and a mental state you've entered into many times before, probably without realizing it. For instance, you've entered a kind of hypnosis while watching television or reading a novel. Hypnotherapists call this *hypnoidal activity*. The difference between hypnoidal activity and hypnotherapy is that in the latter, the objective is to enter the state purposefully and to utilize this mental muscle to obtain practical benefit. As to whether someone can "trick" you into using a muscle (mental or otherwise) presents an interesting topic. For instance, are the producers of television purposefully leading you into hypnoidal activity in order to sell you products they advertise? Can a political leader utilize knowledge about mental states to influence listeners during a speech? The answers could fill another book. But remember this:

Your ability to be hypnotized is part skill and part talent.

A skill is something you learn and practice. A talent is something for which you have natural ability. The good news is that virtually everybody has a certain degree of talent for hypnosis, so it is very likely that you are hypnotizable!

To illustrate this, the skill and talent to be hypnotized may be aptly compared to musical ability. Most people have some talent, even if it remains latent, to play a musical instrument. With opportunity and practice, these people can become proficient or even excellent musicians. A few people are so gifted in music that they can, with little practice or prompting, astound listeners with their excellent abilities. However, there are a few people who are tone deaf, with no musical talent and for whom no amount of practice will ever lead to success in musical endeavors.

In regard to hypnosis, you're probably like most people, in that you have some ability to be hypnotized. But just how adept you become at entering that state depends largely on your level of interest and how much you practice. It is possible that you are one of the gifted—someone who can be quickly, easily, and deeply hypnotized. If you were to go to a stage-hypnosis show, the hypnotist would be on the lookout for you, as you would become the star of the show. You'd be legendary in that you could go deeply into states of hypnosis without the practice most other people would require. A few people have absolutely no innate disposition for hypnosis; they cannot be hypnotized at all, even if they repeatedly make the attempt. An inability to be hypnotized can sometimes be traced to a mental or psychological disorder or to the influence of some mind-altering substances. Thankfully, that's rare.

Again, you are likely to be a person with some talent with hypnosis. And you can develop that skill to be hypnotized and go as deep and as far as your innate talent will permit. "How far is that?" you may ask. Well, you may be able to delve into the deepest hypnotic states, or you may only be able to reach a light state of hypnosis. But the great news is this:

A light or medium state of hypnosis is all that is required for success with most improvement goals!

What this means for you is that unless you are in the tiny minority of those who don't respond at all to hypnosis, you can be hypnotized to achieve your goals as long as you are motivated to succeed! How easily and how deeply you are hypnotized will depend upon your determination and practice. But the chances are excellent that you will achieve success on your very first attempt and that you will get better and better at it in very little time.

Deep-Trance Hypnosis

Before moving on, I do want to make mention of the issue of deep levels of hypnosis, or what might be termed *deep-trance hypnosis*. Like mesmerism, it has engendered a lot of confusion and fear, so I feel compelled to mention it and to clear the air. There are some very deep states of hypnosis, and one of them is referred to by hypnotherapists as *somnambulism*. In fact, it is this state that the media loves to glamorize and which has come to epitomize hypnosis for a great number of people. But here's what you need to know. There are some people who are very good at going into a very deep state of hypnosis. In hypnotherapy, we call these folks *somnambulists* because they enter the state of somnambulism readily and easily.

Somnambulists, while in this deep-trance state, can produce remarkable phenomena not possible at lighter levels of hypnosis. They respond extremely well to almost any nonthreatening suggestion given to them. They can be regressed to any age, remember almost anything that's ever happened to them, relive memories, and control autonomic body functions. They can also be given posthypnotic suggestions of an unusual nature and be completely unaware of what has happened to them while hypnotized. They are the stuff of legends. And I've actually had a few in my private practice over the years. Oh, they are so much fun…a hypnotist's dream. They are also rare! It is estimated that fewer than 2 percent of the population are capable of reaching *somnambulism*. In years of private practice, having hypnotized hundreds of people, I've seen only a dozen or so of them.

The stage hypnotist wants you to believe that everyone on stage enters into a somnambulistic level of hypnosis, but this is usually not the case. If the audience is big enough, however, there is a good chance that there will be several somnambulists present. And it won't take the trained hypnotist long to find these folks. And if he does, there will be a show of shows…everything you expected of a hypnotist. What's funny, though, is that any moderately proficient hypnotist can place a somnambulist into deep trance with very little effort. These people tend to be extremely susceptible to suggestion. Their ability lies mostly in them, not in the hypnotist, though the stage performer would have you believe otherwise.

Many people have often been left to believe that somnambulism is the only true hypnosis. That's like thinking that the only way to be under water is to plummet to a depth of twenty thousand leagues. Hypnosis is a relative condition, but many people don't understand this, which leads to false expectations. To illustrate, I remember recently fielding a phone call from a man who said that he wanted me to put him "under." I asked him what he meant by "under." He explained that he'd visited three other hypnotists and none of them could hypnotize him at all. He wanted to be "unconscious…really hypnotized." I tried, as I am doing here, to explain that deep-trance hypnosis is somewhat rare and not needed (or desirable, for that matter) for self-improvement goals. But he insisted that unless he was "out," it was not real hypnosis. I turned away his patronage, for I knew he would be unlikely to derive benefit from my hypnotic services. It's not that I didn't think I could hypnotize him. But I knew his strong disbelief in lighter levels of hypnosis (based on some stage show he saw, no doubt) would block any hypnotic suggestions from taking effect.

I'm telling you these things so that you don't fall into that same trap. The reality is that most hypnotized subjects do not enter deep trances. They do, however, enter into very useful relative states of heightened suggestion, totally adequate for helping them reach their goals. And in terms of therapeutic hypnosis, that's really the name of the game.

Hypnosis, Meditation, and the Alpha State

A lot of people ask me to tell them the difference between self-hypnosis and meditation. Are they the same thing? The reason it can be misleading to give a straight answer is that ways of defining both terms are broad. It depends how you define self-hypnosis and meditation as to whether they can be considered identical. So we'll use my definition of *hypnosis* (given earlier) for argument's sake. That is, that hypnosis is a condition of narrowed attention in which suggestibility is heightened. Now comes an equally tricky matter of pinning down a definition for meditation, for there are many types of meditation. If you mean by *meditation* the kind that is performed in silence or with a mantra in which the aim is the quieting of the waters of the thinking process, then there are similarities and distinct differences between meditation and hypnosis. I'd say that the technique of this kind of meditation does place the meditator, arguably, into a hypnotic state. But the main difference is that the purpose of hypnosis is very different from this kind of meditation. Hypnosis has as its aim not the mere quieting of thought but the utilization of that mental condition to deliver desired suggestions to the subconscious. The meditator, on the other hand, derives benefit by the condition of the quieted mind all by itself. Hypnosis, therefore, has a specific end as its goal; whereas the meditator has no such specific end in mind other than an uplifting feeling and a lasting sense of calm and contentment that result from the regular practice of this art.

There are, however, other kinds of meditation. One of them is known as *active meditation*. In this form of meditation, one relaxes the body and enters into a state of meditation with a specific goal or intent in mind. This kind of meditation is virtually identical with my definition of hypnosis. The only difference is what it's called and, perhaps, the techniques used to arrive at the intended condition.

In addition to hypnosis, many people ask whether "creative visualization" can be considered hypnosis. The answer is yes, that it usually is a form of hypnosis. The kind of creative visualization made popular by Shakti Gawain tells people to relax their bodies from head to toe before they begin to visualize specific images that are intended to direct their inner minds to create change from within and without. The relaxed condition invariably produces a relative state of heightened suggestibility, and the imagery tends to create and sustain the focus of the practitioner. I think it is wise, for the most part, that proponents of creative visualization do not inform participants of its relationship to hypnosis.

Why? Because even though hypnosis has become more widely known and accepted over the years, there's still a lot of fear surrounding the term *hypnosis*. By creating or developing terms that do not mention hypnosis but that do the same thing, they avoid possible mental blocks which may otherwise arise in their readers or pupils. In fact, you are to be commended for venturing to read this book and totally dissolve and fears you might have had in regard to being hypnotized. I had a metaphysical teacher many years ago who taught pupils how to enter "The Silence" before engaging in metaphysical meditation. Eventually, he revealed that "The Silence" was a euphemism for *self-hypnosis*, but he didn't wish to generate fear by using that term until we were ready to handle it.

Also, some people who have studied mind-control methods that attempt to train pupils to enter an alpha brain-wave level have asked me whether the alpha state and hypnosis are the same thing. But here we go again—it depends on definitions and the uses for which these phenomena are intended. It would be accurate to say that one who enters into an alpha state—a state of bodily relaxation in which the mind becomes focused and susceptible to learning—is definitely experiencing a level of hypnosis. However, it is not true that hypnosis always takes place in an alpha state. Hypnosis often does include the slowing of the brain waves, though it cannot be said that this is always the case. It is also true that hypnosis can take place in an even slower brain-wave level, known as *the theta level*. So let's just say that the alpha state and hypnosis often overlap but are not one and the same thing.

How Traditional Hypnotherapy Works

Although there are many methods therapists use to hypnotize their clients, sessions generally follow a similar format. Generally there are four steps involved:

Step 1: Relaxation. The session begins with some form of relaxation for body and mind to prepare the person for hypnosis. The most common technique is that of progressive relaxation, in which the person concentrates and relaxes the body, one muscle group at a time, until his entire body is calmed. All by itself this usually induces a light hypnotic state. When the body relaxes, the conscious mind automatically relaxes and therefore becomes more receptive to suggestion.

Step 2: "Going Under." Following relaxation, the next step is the hypnotic-induction phase. The induction is designed to place the individual being hypnotized in as deep of a state of hypnosis as possible. There are dozens of possible induction methods. Some of them involve some sort of monotonous physical movement. An example is the well-known swinging pendulum method, in which a person gazes intensely at a shiny bauble. This is a valid induction technique, but there are many other methods available. Other common induction techniques merely require the person being hypnotized to visualize a relaxing scene described by the therapist.

All of the induction methods have one thing in common. They are all designed to distract, misdirect, or suspend the critical factor of the mind. The "critical factor" is a name given to the security system discussed in Chapter One, which filters information before it is accepted by the subconscious mind. It allows certain suggestions and ideas to go into the inner chamber of the mind while rejecting others.

The hypnotic induction is a way to temporarily subdue the critical factor so that the subconscious readily accepts subsequent suggestions. It's important to note that with very few exceptions, the hypnotized subject remains completely aware throughout the hypnotic induction and hears the therapist's voice clearly. The subject does not become unconscious during the induction. In fact, awareness intensifies during the procedure.

Step 3: Hypnotic Suggestions. After the hypnotic induction, the therapist begins imparting therapeutic hypnotic suggestions. These suggestions are in accord with the person's stated goal and are ideally phrased in such a way as to have maximum impact upon the subconscious mind. Some suggestions are very direct, such as, "You are now a nonsmoker." Other types of suggestion take an indirect or subtle approach and may include anecdotes, metaphors, and imagery.

Some people worry that hypnotic suggestions will make them act or feel like a robot—that they'll become a helpless puppet of the hypnotist. But they have the capability to resist any hypnotic suggestion. It is assumed, however, that the suggestions given to them while in hypnosis are designed to help them so they will want to follow them. Stage shows can lead them to believe that the hypnotist might embarrass them, but a good hypnotherapist will never give subjects suggestions designed to embarrass or trouble them in any way.

Step 4: Return to Total Wakefulness. Finally, the person is "awakened" from hypnosis. This is not the same as being awakened from sleep but is simply a return from the hypnotic state to normal, everyday consciousness. There is no danger of being unable to awaken from hypnosis. In fact, the word *awaken* is slightly misleading. It might be truer to say that one simply "returns" from hypnosis to an everyday state of consciousness.

The Trouble with Traditional Hypnotherapy

The problems associated with traditional hypnotherapy can be summed up in two words: *time* and *money*.

As with many services, you will have to take time out of your schedule to set an appointment and travel to your area hypnotherapist. A single hypnosis session takes about an hour, and it is common for therapies to take three or more sessions. All of those things add up to a significant time commitment. Perhaps if you only have one goal—one area of self-improvement for which you need hypnosis—it may be well worth the time to drive to the therapist, undergo the hypnosis session, drive back to work or home, and repeat the process until the problem is solved. But what if you have several goals you wish to meet using hypnosis? Do you have the time for that many sessions?

There is also the issue of expense. Private hypnosis sessions do not come cheaply. They can be as costly or even more so than a trip to the doctor. Session rates vary widely, with some hypnotherapists charging far more than one hundred dollars for a single session! Now, if money is no object, then please give your local hypnotherapists a call. We'll gladly take your money in exchange for our time, knowledge, and expertise.

If time and money are issues for you, self-hypnosis is a great alternative. It will not only better fit your schedule and budget—it will empower you. When you become your own hypnotist, you don't have to rely on anyone else to meet your self-improvement goals.

Self-Hypnosis for Self-Improvement

The concept of self-hypnosis is bewildering to some people. But hypnosis isn't really something that is done to you. It is a process that is facilitated by the hypnotist. The ability to be hypnotized does not depend so much on the hypnotist as it does on the person being hypnotized. And by now, you understand that hypnosis is conducted while you maintain control of your mental faculties. Therefore, it should not come as a surprise that you are capable of entering hypnosis while remaining awake and aware so that you may supply your inner mind with your own suggestions. The term *self-hypnosis* refers to a person entering a hypnotic state with no outside assistance. Virtually anyone can develop this skill and use it to maximum benefit.

Like regular hypnosis, self-hypnosis is an ability which is part talent and part skill. Proficiency with self-hypnosis is based on aptitude, knowledge, and practice. Once developed, this ability can propel you faster and easier toward any and all of your self-improvement goals.

How Traditional Self-Hypnosis Works

Traditional methods of self-hypnosis are similar to those of hypnosis administered by a professional therapist, except that the individual performs all phases without assistance. The format of self-hypnosis sessions vary but the two types usually contain overlapping procedures.

First, the subject relaxes using an effective process such as progressive relaxation, as previously described. This is done with the eyes closed, as is the remainder of the session. Once relaxed, the person induces the hypnotic state using a predetermined method, often involving the use of visual imagery.

Once in the desired state of self-hypnosis, the suggestion portion of the session starts. The person silently speaks to her subconscious, giving it a set of preestablished suggestions. These suggestions can take on a variety of forms—including silent verbal suggestions, affirmations, or the use of imaginary scenes—all in order to convey the desired directives to the inner mind. After the suggestions have been imparted satisfactorily, the individual uses an awakening procedure to come back to ordinary consciousness.

The Pitfalls of Traditional Self-Hypnosis

There are at least three potential pitfalls when using traditional methods of self-hypnosis. They get in the way of that person successfully hypnotizing himself. Before you hypnotize yourself in the standard way, you must (at the very least) study hypnotic procedure and understand how to formulate effective suggestions. This is a huge pitfall, and the reason is obvious. If you are a busy person or if you're lacking patience, you may find yourself tossing the standard self-hypnosis book aside before ever applying the knowledge and techniques!

At least this is what many people do—not only with self-hypnosis books, but with most self-improvement programs. We have desire and good intentions. We go out and buy a book or program. We start reading…and we might even learn a little. But time constraints and a society-driven expectation for instant gratification cause us to abandon our efforts before we put anything we've learned into practice.

A second pitfall of traditional self-hypnosis is that it requires preparation and memorization. Before you begin any self-hypnosis sessions, it's essential that you prepare and memorize the techniques and suggestions you'll use because, after all, your eyes will be closed! So not only must you spend time learning how to formulate suggestions and techniques, you must also put in the time and quite a bit of effort to memorize them!

Finally, the most common and perhaps the most troubling of the potential pitfalls of traditional self-hypnosis methods is when you, as the subject, accidentally fall asleep. Because hypnosis induces a state of relaxation, it's very easy to fall asleep before having the opportunity to impart your memorized suggestions to your inner mind. Even when you manage to stay awake, it is equally common to find yourself so relaxed that you forget your memorized suggestions or even why you hypnotized yourself at all!

What You Should Know about Hypnosis—Summary

- Hypnosis is a process whereby the mind enters a relative state of heightened suggestibility.
- This state can be achieved through a variety of ways…and most people experience it on a regular basis though they may be unaware of it.
- The hypnotic state can be used to impart helpful and beneficial suggestions to the inner mind for self-change.
- Virtually everyone is hypnotizable, but the ability to be hypnotized is based partly on talent, partly on skill.
- Self-hypnosis allows anyone to become his own hypnotist, but there are some potential pitfalls involved with the traditional form of self-hypnosis.

3

How I Discovered
Instant Self-Hypnosis

As you will learn in this chapter, the concept of "eyes-open" hypnosis is not new. What is new is my discovery of a specific eyes-open method of self-hypnosis involving the reading and writing of hypnotic scripts. The discovery was a complete fluke and occurred very early in my career as a hypnotherapist. There were actually two discoveries, one dealing with reading and the other with writing. This chapter explains how I accidentally hypnotized myself while reading and why it's an important breakthrough for self-improvement.

Eyes-Open Hypnosis Is Common

Before I reveal my amazing discovery, you should realize that there is actually nothing new about being hypnotized with your eyes open. It's something you've experienced in various forms and degrees in your life. For example, have you ever been driving along a straight road late at night on a journey that takes an hour? You might have found yourself watching the dotted white line that divides the lanes of the highway. The way the lines seemed to pass by caught your eyes and unintentionally fascinated you. You kept looking at it, for it is where your eyes were naturally drawn. And in what seemed to be only five minutes, you realized you reached your destination. It dawned on you that an entire hour had passed. The road literally fascinated you; it hypnotized you. And the sense of time distortion is a sure and common sign of hypnosis.

There are other examples of eyes-open hypnosis even more common. If you go to the movies, you enter into a dark theater and watch a moving picture, which is actually a series of flashing pictures that pass before your eyes. If it's a good movie, you find yourself caught up in the plot. If it's a thriller, you even find your heart racing and a genuine sense of fear, even though you know it's only a movie and that you are perfectly safe. What's happening there? Yep, it's a kind of hypnosis.

And it is a good illustration of what hypnosis can do. In the theater experience, you actually hope that you will get caught up emotionally in the movie. You invest your time and your money and your intention in order to feel and experience something. And sure enough, if the movie is even halfway decent, you do find yourself thinking and feeling as though what is on screen is actually taking place. You even start to identify with the characters so much that your body makes your heart race, fills you with adrenaline, gets you excited or angry.

That's exactly the kind of thing hypnosis can do. First, it needs your cooperation to be effective. You have to want to be hypnotized, and you also have to want the change or improvement that hypnosis can help you to get. You have to invest in the idea and the therapy. You open yourself up to the experience. When you do, the suggestions have an effect not only on your mind in some sort of abstract way but also on your body and how it reacts to certain kinds of stimuli. For example, if you are hypnotizing yourself in order to get over your fear of public speaking, you will give yourself suggestions of a positive nature having to do with your reactions when speaking in public. When the mind accepts the hypnotic suggestions, your body will actually behave differently the next time you are in front of others and have to speak. You will find that you feel calmer—that your body is no longer making your palms sweat, your heart pound, etc. It doesn't matter if you don't consciously understand how the mind is able to get the body to do that any more than you need to understand how it releases adrenaline during a thriller in the theater. Leave that to your subconscious. But instruct it through hypnosis what you want it to do, how you want it to react in specific situations, and then expect the changes to materialize.

A Discovery "Hidden in Plain Sight"

One of my two Instant Self-Hypnosis discoveries occurred when I accidentally hypnotized myself while reading out loud! One evening I was reading a hypnosis script, rehearsing my delivery for a hypnotic audio program to be recorded for a subject the next day. The written monologue contained all of the elements common to traditional hypnosis methodology, including a progressive relaxation portion, a visualization-based induction, therapeutic suggestions, and a wake-up to rouse the subject out of hypnosis.

As I read aloud in a soft, lulling voice, my senses were suddenly shocked alert by the very shrill ringing of the telephone. As the phone rang a second time, it seemed abrasive and disquieting to me like never before. I realized that I had somehow entered into a state of sensory hypersensitivity. Professional hypnotherapists refer to this state as *atmospheric hyperacuity*, which occurs when a hypnotized person reaches a certain level of hypnotic trance. Feeling that surge of irritation rush through my nervous system, I looked up from the script I was reading. Looking about the office, I had a strange sensation, as though the room were at a tilt—kind of the way the archvillains' lairs on the old *Batman* series used to appear. It was subtle but noticeable. Everything felt a little distant in the room, almost as though it was an illusion or a projection. This, too, I recognized as a familiar signpost of hypnosis. It's the feeling I had experienced many times just after private hypnosis sessions with my clients; anyone who hypnotizes others for a living will tell you that they become accidentally self-hypnotized quite often (or always!) as they perform their service. Why?

Well, think about it for a moment. As a hypnosis session begins, the therapist can hear the sound of his or her own voice while assisting the hypnotic subject into a deep state of relaxation with very calming tones and imagery. Then the dialogue continues in order to place the client into a pronounced hypnotic state. And as the therapist watches the subject get more and more relaxed, this acts as what is called an "indirect suggestion," which often makes the therapist become even more relaxed. Plus, if relaxing hypnotic-type music is played during the session, the therapist hears it just as surely as the hypnotic subject does. All of these factors predictably lead the therapist into a state of hypnosis right along with the client! I've recognized this for many years now. And it is similar to the experience I had as I read from my hypnotic script. It was then that I realized I had accidentally hypnotized myself with my eyes open while reading my hypnosis script aloud!

The discovery made perfect sense to me as a clinical hypnotherapist. There I was, reading aloud, as the calming sound of my own speaking voice washed over me. Simultaneously, I had been reading a narrative specifically designed to hypnotize. So I was hearing my own hypnotic voice while listening to my words, carefully phrased to induce hypnosis.

But how was it possible I had managed to enter this state with my eyes open? There was nothing in my hypnosis training and education to verify this discovery as a viable induction method. Conventional sources teach that it is possible to reach a hypnotic state and, given significant depth of trance, to open the eyes while remaining in that condition. But none of my books or professors ever mentioned entering hypnosis with the eyes open while reading a hypnotic script, nor had any of my instructors mentioned it.

I wondered how the experts of hypnosis had overlooked such a simple method of hypnotic induction. I could only speculate that the technique was so obvious that it had been hidden in plain sight. Another way to look at it was that the professionals might have been fully aware of the method, but they might have been afraid of its simplicity and how it might put them out of business. After all, if almost anyone can enter hypnosis just by reading a professional hypnotic script, why spend big bucks going to a hypnotherapist? Both explanations are plausible. Regardless of the reason for their silence, I knew I had made an amazing discovery:

Reading a hypnosis script out loud hypnotizes its reader!

I already knew from education and experience that entering a hypnosislike state almost always occurs while watching a movie or reading a compelling novel. And I already recognized that while administering hypnotherapy, I frequently entered into a light trance state along with my clients, and I would do this with my eyes open. But what was new to me was that I had stumbled onto a way to induce hypnosis by merely reading a hypnotic narrative and could therefore use that state to impart inner mind therapy.

That's exactly what I began to do, and I found this method works, for I began using it for my own self-improvement goals. I applied it to things like weight loss, and I dropped ten pounds in five weeks. I used it to overcome procrastination and got my bills paid on time—miracle of miracles. I improved my tennis game with added concentration. I used it to increase my income. I even used it to help me write and complete this book. The results were rapid and often superior to the results I'd achieved using traditional self-hypnosis.

Advantages over Traditional Self-Hypnosis

While putting my discovery into practice for my own self-improvement goals, I realized that this method had clear advantages over traditional methods of self-hypnosis. To start with, this method allows the eyes to remain open at all times, so the potential pitfall of falling asleep during self-hypnosis is eliminated. This ensures completion of the therapeutic suggestions, which is the most important part of self-hypnosis.

Having your eyes open also bypasses another of the pitfalls of traditional self-hypnosis—the need for preparation. All of the suggestions are written down and are spoken out loud while reading. No memorization is required. Plus, when reading a prepared hypnosis script like the ones in this book, the professional script supplies the complete therapy, from beginning to end.

Finally, with this method you don't have to have knowledge regarding hypnotic procedures and hypnotic suggestion. You can simply read a professionally written hypnosis script out loud to your-self to enter hypnosis and receive full benefit from the therapeutic suggestions!

Literacy and the ability to speak are the only prerequisite skills required for using this method to hypnotize yourself.

An Innovation in Self-Hypnosis Methodology

When I noticed such practically applied and rapid successes, I realized that I had uncovered an innovative, breakthrough approach to self-hypnosis from which many people might benefit. I began experi-menting and refining the procedure to make it as simple, quick, and easy as possible for any literate individual to utilize. I named the method "Instant Self-Hypnosis" because it requires no knowledge of hypnosis, can be applied immediately, and works quickly.

How I Discovered Instant Self-Hypnosis—Summary

- A state of eyes-open hypnosis is achievable through the recitation of a professional hypnotherapeutic script or narrative designed for that purpose.
- This method has distinct advantages over traditional self-hypnosis, advantages which make it easier to use and virtually foolproof. I named the method "Instant Self-Hypnosis."

4

Experiencing Instant Self-Hypnosis for Yourself

In this chapter, you will get hands-on experience with Instant Self-Hypnosis. First, you'll learn the how and why of the method. Then you will be led through an exercise that lays down the foundation for all future success with the method. After this, you'll be ready to apply Instant Self-Hypnosis to your specific needs and goals.

The Method: How and Why It Works

With the basic method of Instant Self-Hypnosis, you will read aloud a narrative called the "Master Induction." This is a script designed to induce hypnosis and establish a state of heightened suggestibility. Once you reach that state, you'll then read beneficial suggestions that are absorbed by your inner mind. After the suggestions, you'll read a "Wake-Up" to bring yourself out of hypnosis and back to everyday awareness.

The modus operandi and principles of this method are really very simple. When reading the "Master Induction" aloud to yourself, you use a lulling tone of voice, appropriate to the narrative. You—the reader—attempt the kind of soothing tone and cadence you might expect from a professional hypnotist.

The sound of your own voice produces a tranquilizing effect on your mind and body. The content of the narrative utilizes multisensory imagery and suggestions that you experience on both conscious and subconscious levels to induce a state of eyes-open hypnosis. Whether you're aware of it or not, your mind cannot help but visualize the images presented in the text. Meanwhile, the conscious mind is misdirected when scanning the lines of the narrative, assisting in the suspension of the critical factor, previously discussed. There are also posthypnotic suggestions in the narrative that prompt you to go deeper and deeper into eyes-open hypnosis each time you use Instant Self-Hypnosis. The combination of your hypnotic voice, the conscious visual scanning of words on the page, and the targeted contents of the "Master Induction" predictably produces a hypnotic state in which you are able to absorb therapeutic suggestions on a subconscious level.

It's important to know that you may not necessarily feel hypnotized during or after an Instant Self-Hypnosis session. Light levels of hypnosis can be hard to recognize, but as I've discussed, their effects can be every bit as therapeutic as deeper states. However, when using the Instant Self-Hypnosis method regularly, there is likely to come a time when you may feel something, such as an evocation of emotions while reading portions of the narrative, an intensity of focus during the session, or a deep sense of relaxation—or all three. Such feelings indicate that you've reached a deeper level of hypnosis than earlier sessions. Your mind is becoming adept at this new skill!

Your First Instant Self-Hypnosis Session

Now it's time for you to actually experience Instant Self-Hypnosis for yourself! This first session does not target personal self-improvement goals. Rather, it's designed as a hypnotic primer for the mind to enhance subsequent experiences when utilizing Instant Self-Hypnosis.

During this session, you will read aloud three things: the "Master Induction," the written suggestions that follow it, and the provided "Wake-Up." The entire procedure takes only about fifteen minutes.

This will initiate you to eyes-open hypnosis and at the same time automatically prepare you to later enter eyes-open self-hypnosis very easily. This narrative lays the foundation for all future success with Instant Self-Hypnosis. So give it your full effort and attention!

Preparation and Reading Instructions

1. Find a quiet place where you can be completely alone and won't be disturbed for fifteen minutes or so.
2. Subdue the room's lighting. There should be enough light to read by, but it should be dim enough to support a calm, contemplative mood.
3. Consider playing some gentle instrumental music in the background. Set it at a low volume.
4. Sit in a comfortable chair or sofa and place the narrative (which follows) on your lap or in front of you. You may hold the book in your hand as you would any other book or you may sit at a table and place the book on the table in front of you.
5. When you're ready to begin, read the "Master Induction" aloud following these guidelines:
   a. Use a gentle, soothing tone of voice.
   b. Read slowly and pause slightly wherever you see the three dots.
   c. Emphasize any italicized words and phrases. It is not necessary to read aloud the words found in parentheses, but be sure to follow directions indicated within them.
   d. Think about what you're reading rather than merely parroting the words.

Important: make sure you read the entire narrative from beginning to end—including the "Wake-Up"—in one sitting.

A Note about Visualization

Some people get hung up because they can't vividly visualize the images described in the narrative. If you're not seeing vivid images, don't worry too much. Visualization is a natural ability of your subconscious mind. It is nothing you have to try to do. Over time you'll get better at it. What's more important is to feel the emotions associated with what you are reading. Leave the visualization part to your subconscious.

Alternative Induction Available

The "Master Induction" includes imagery of a modern building and an elevator. If you are someone who detests modern architecture or is afraid of elevators, there is an alternative induction available to you in Appendix A. The imagery of the alternative induction is that of a majestic castle and a carpeted stairway, which you may find more pleasing.

The Master Induction

(to be read aloud)

"Feeling a sense of privacy and comfort, I allow the sound of my own voice to soothe my mind and body, while I speak slowly and softly. My body is slowing *down* as though everything is moving in slow motion. With every word I read and every sound I utter, I feel *more relaxed* and at peace. Moment by moment, my mind is becoming as *clear* as the surface of a calm and quiet mountain lake.

"As my mind clears, I use my imagination to *relax more deeply* while I read. I imagine that I am sitting on a comfortable chair on a beautiful beach as I read. With my peripheral vision I see the golden sand that surrounds me…and the waves as they crash on the shore. I hear the gentle and rhythmic sounds they make.

"I feel a moist sea breeze waft over my body. I notice the warm sun on my skin. I feel its golden touch on my scalp, allowing me to let go of any excess tension there. All of my thoughts seem to *quiet down now* as I concentrate my attention on the sun's warmth on my face…on my cheeks…on my ears—and around my jaw.

"The healing light seems to caress my neck and warm my throat, allowing the words to flow easily and effortlessly from my mouth. It feels as though hundreds of tiny fingers of light are massaging my shoulders and my upper back as I relax—waves of warmth and relaxation cascade down…down my arms and out through my fingers.

"I mentally scan my hips, pelvis, and buttocks…and let any tension or anxiety there be gently washed away by a stream of light. I become aware of my legs now…they are almost aglow as sunlight floods down through them. My legs feel so relaxed. Even my feet and toes *feel warm* and comfortable…warm and comfortable now.

"As I bask in the glorious sun, I imagine closing my eyes as I prepare to hypnotize myself. I draw three slow deep breaths (draw three deep breaths). For a few moments I can see the glow of orange light through my closed eyelids. But now that light fades into a comforting darkness as I draw my attention inward…inward…toward the center of my mind.

"I imagine that I am approaching a beautiful, tall, and modern building. I walk through the revolving door and step into a beautiful lobby. Inside the building stands a strong, armed security guard who keeps the building safe from intruders. The guard looks at me with a steely glare but then recognizes me as the owner of the building. The guard works for me. I give the guard a satisfied nod and make my way toward the elevator.

"I see the reflection of myself in the mirrorlike surface of the elevator doors. I look relaxed and sure of myself. I press the down arrow and the doors of the elevator open. *I feel very safe* as I step into a spacious and luxurious elevator car. I turn toward the panel of buttons which indicate the floor numbers. I press the number ten to take me ten floors down beneath ground level. The number ten lights up and the elevator doors close. The elevator car begins to move down smoothly through the long, deep elevator shaft…with a very gentle humming sound. I watch the numbered lights above the door as they change. Each number lights up for a moment as the elevator moves past the indicated floor. As the numbers change…one by one…I feel myself descending to a wonderful place within myself…far beneath the surface.

"One…I watch the numbers as the elevator moves down…I relax deeper with every number.

"Two…going down beneath the surface of this great structure…deeper below the surface.

"Three…by the time I reach the tenth number, I will be deeply *hypnotized.*

"Four…I will be *hypnotized* with my cycs open…open to helpful suggestions.

"Five…I feel myself descending…smoothly…effortlessly. I feel deeper a peace.

"Six…still watching the number change above the door…one by one, as the elevator goes down.

"Seven…going *deeper now*…feeling tranquil and very relaxed now.

"Eight…I am safe…I feel calm…going down…down…deeper *down.*

"Nine…I allow myself to easily enter into hypnosis with my eyes open now.

"Ten…the elevator comes to a slow stop. I see the number ten light up above the door. I have arrived. I am *now hypnotized.*

"As the doors open, I enter into a comfortably furnished reading room. A burning log in the fireplace crackles and blazes brightly, as though welcoming me into the chamber. I approach a very comfortable-looking chair and sit down. I pick up a book on a small table next to the chair. I read the cover of the book which says *Instant Self-Hypnosis.* I open the book and begin to read. The words address me directly and seem to jump off of the pages and into my mind. And here is what they say:

"'You are now hypnotized with your eyes open. Every time you read any induction from this book of Instant Self-Hypnosis, you automatically enter a relaxed state of body and mind. And each time you hypnotize yourself with Instant Self-Hypnosis, you will automatically go deeper into hypnosis than the time that came before. You will now awaken yourself from hypnosis by reading the 'Wake-Up.'"

(The Wake-Up)

"I will awaken from hypnosis by counting to five. When I reach the number five, I will become fully alert and wide awake. One…beginning to awaken from hypnosis. Two…becoming aware of my surroundings…feeling satisfied, safe, and comfortable. Three…looking forward to positive results from this hypnosis session. Four…feeling optimistic and refreshed. FIVE…FIVE…FIVE…now wide awake and fully alert."

Examining Your Experience

Congratulations! If you followed the directions and read the "Master Induction" script aloud, then you successfully hypnotized yourself! You may or may not have felt hypnotized. You may or may not have been aware of mental or physiological changes. But that's not important at this time. As noted earlier, the "feeling" or awareness of being hypnotized may take several sessions to generate. Rest assured that if you read the script out loud in a soothing voice in an undisturbed environment, you entered a state of eyes-open hypnosis. And remember, even a light state of hypnosis can be very effective for imparting suggestions to your subconscious and for initiating monumental changes in your life. The feeling of hypnosis is only an indicator of a particular depth of hypnosis and is not always present in the lighter levels.

Being Convinced You Were Hypnotized

With Instant Self-Hypnosis, you may find yourself stumbling over or slurring some of the words as you read them. Should that happen to you, consider it a welcome signpost that you've reached a particular depth of the hypnotic state. Slurring of words, intense focus, strong emotions, or other signposts that you are hypnotized may make themselves known to you as you use Instant Self-Hypnosis more and more. Such evidence of the stages of hypnosis may be termed *convincers* by some professional hypnotherapists. With Instant Self-Hypnosis, convincers are not something to be sought to prove anything to you. Rather when they do occur, they simply reinforce what you already know to be true: that you can achieve a state of hypnosis while reading.

Instant Self-Hypnosis for Your Goals

Once you've read the "Master Induction" in this chapter, your mind is conditioned to enter a state of greater suggestibility every time you use Instant Self-Hypnosis. You do not need to read the "Master Induction" again. Instead, you will recite one of two other inductions found in parts two and three of this book. They are virtually identical to the "Master Induction" except that instead of promptly awakening you from hypnosis, they direct you to stay in hypnosis while you impart therapeutic suggestions pertinent to your goals.

Experiencing Instant Self-Hypnosis for Yourself—Summary

- The "Master Induction," when read aloud, produces a state of hypnosis and heightened suggestibility. It also conditions the mind to enter a deeper state of hypnosis upon each reading of any induction in this book.
- You may or may not feel hypnotized during or after reading the "Master Induction," but the feeling is not important.
- Assurance of the validity of and success with Instant Self-Hypnosis comes as you put the method to use for personal goals and experience your desired changes.

Part Two

5

Thirty-Five Instant Self-Hypnosis Scripts

In this section, you are offered thirty-five professionally prepared Instant Self-Hypnosis scripts to accommodate a variety of common self-improvement goals. It is probable that you already know exactly which self-improvement goal is most pressing in your life at this time. It is wise to begin working on the self-improvement goal that motivates you the most, since motivation is the prime factor for success in all forms of hypnotherapy and self-help.

How to Use Instant Self-Hypnosis Scripts

Review the Instant Self-Hypnosis script titles to see which, if any, match your current goals. If none of the professional scripts matches the goals you've set for yourself, do not despair. In Part Three, you'll be able to easily write your own script and customize it for virtually any goal!

Follow these steps to utilize the Instant Self-Hypnosis scripts in this chapter:

1. Select one script to work with per session. Find the prepared script suited to your goal and bookmark it before beginning.
2. When you are ready to start, find a quiet place where you won't be disturbed for twenty minutes or so. Lighting should be soft as opposed to harsh but bright enough so you can read.
3. Sit in a comfortable chair or sofa and place the book in a comfortable position for reading and turning the pages.
4. If you wish, you may play some quiet instrumental music in the background, but keep the volume low. Make sure the music is

calming rather than dynamic. Soothing environmental sounds are also acceptable.

5. Begin the session by reading the Instant Self-Hypnosis "Reader's Induction" aloud. You'll notice that it is almost identical to the "Master Induction" but has been edited slightly to leave room for the self-improvement suggestions found in the prepared scripts. Read slowly with a relaxed tone of voice.

6. At the end of the induction, follow the prompt and turn to the bookmarked script. Continue to read out loud all of the written suggestions in the script. Read them slowly and feel the importance of their meaning. Use expression and emotion in your voice rather than the lulling tone you used during the induction. Use extra vocal emphasis on any italicized words or phrases. You need not read aloud the words written in parentheses, but do follow their directions.

7. Once you've read all of the suggestions in the script, end your session by reading the "Wake-Up" aloud. Even without doing this, you would slowly and naturally come out of hypnosis on your own. But to awaken quickly and efficiently from each hypnosis session, use the "Wake-Up," which you'll find after every Instant Self-Hypnosis script. The "Wake-Up" is repeated as both a reminder and for your convenience.

Remember, select only one goal per Instant Self-Hypnosis session. If you have several self-improvement goals, conduct separate Instant Self-Hypnosis sessions for each. You may choose, for example, a session in the morning for smoking cessation then one in the evening for weight loss.

Planning to Work on Your Goal

Once you've decided on which goal you would like to begin working toward, briefly take a look at the script corresponding to it before you begin your first session. Beneath the title for the goal you will find a brief explanation as to what the script is designed for—what issues it addresses. Be sure to read it and see that it speaks directly to your needs, and check out at least a few of the suggestions to see whether they are appropriate to you. If they aren't, you can always write your own suggestions as you will be taught in Part Three of this book. Don't worry if one or two of the suggestions don't seem to directly target your concerns, as any suggestion your mind recognizes as not applicable will be easily disregarded by your subconscious.

Before you begin reading the "Reader's Induction," it is a good idea to think about why you want to reach the goal you've set for yourself. While the scripts address motivations to some extent, it is important that you get to the root emotion surrounding the desire to achieve your selected goal. Make sure that you really want what you say you want and that you're not making excuses for yourself. For instance, if you want to stop smoking, make sure you've really come to grips with how harmful it is to you…how smoking no longer serves any useful purpose. If you are still thinking about how much you are going to miss your precious cigarettes, then you are not ready to stop smoking, and no amount of hypnosis is going to help you. The motivation must be complete, genuine, and heartfelt. What is it, for instance, that you are after on an emotional level when you reach your goal? What will you get out of achieving success? Is it a feeling of accomplishment? Self-pride? Liberation? Self-satisfaction? Vanity?

There's no wrong motivation when it comes to self-improvement. This is your life, so be honest with yourself about your true motivation. It may even be helpful before you begin the session to write down all of the reasons why you want success with your goal. Writing down the motivations will help clarify them in your own mind. Even if you think the motivation is obvious, take the time to clarify it for yourself anyway. It will only take a few minutes at most and will propel you to success more quickly.

Looking for Results

You may wonder after you begin putting Instant Self-Hypnosis into practice just what to expect. When and how will the results begin to manifest? Although results will vary from person to person as to when and how they materialize, there are some general signs to look for. As to when you will begin to see results, there should be a noticeable difference in your attitude or behavior within about three to five applications, on average. That is, after you've repeated your Instant Self-Hypnosis sessions using the same script three to five times on consecutive days, you will probably begin to notice a partial or total improvement. For some people, only one or two applications are needed to see wonderful results. Even if that is the case for you, it is recommended that you continue to apply Instant Self-Hypnosis for your goal seven times to be sure the results are long-lasting. In other cases, people have needed up to twelve applications to get satisfactory results. Remember that unlike drugs, which often follow the law of diminishing returns, where it takes more and more of the drug to get the same effect, hypnosis works in the reverse way. The more you reinforce it, the stronger and longer-lasting the effects tend to be. Don't underestimate the power of repetition. Remember, this will only take you about fifteen or twenty minutes per application. So there isn't a big-time commitment required. And don't assume because you didn't stop smoking or pass up the donuts after your first application that it won't happen later on. Days or weeks later, for no reason you can figure, the suggestions might suddenly kick in and you will get what you wanted!

There are, of course, goals for which the effects are more subtle and take longer to see. For instance, the abundance script called "Make More Money" may take time to manifest results. The suggestions of that script work on subconsciously held beliefs about money and, even when they change, it will still take time for life circumstances to alter so that you find yourself in positions to take advantage of your newfound beliefs. So some goals will take more time to manifest. With a little common sense, you'll know which ones they are.

And what about when there's no effect at all...even after seven, twelve...even fourteen applications using the same script? Will Instant Self-Hypnosis always work? I don't know any therapy that always works for everyone...not even aspirin for headaches works all the time for everyone, right? But should you not get the result you wanted, remember this axiom: there is no such thing as failure—there are only results. Did Edison fail hundreds of times to invent the light bulb, or did he just have hundreds of results that didn't satisfy him? If the results aren't there, consider changing tactics. Think about your goal again. Check the script to make sure it covers your goal in the way that you desire. If it doesn't, you should try writing your own suggestions. In some cases, you may need to break down the goal into smaller parts. If that's the case, this book teaches you an easy way to write your own suggestions as you are hypnotized!

Ready for Success

Now you are ready to begin using any professional Instant Self-Hypnosis script. You may be surprised how effective this method is in propelling you toward your desired goals.

Each of the professionally prepared scripts I've written for you includes several kinds of suggestion. It is not important at this time that you understand the types of suggestion or how they work. But most of the scripts are nearly identical to the suggestions I give clients who come to me for one-on-one hypnotherapy sessions. They've proven highly effective for quick and lasting results.

Finally, plan to enjoy your Instant Self-Hypnosis sessions! You should find them fun as well as beneficial. In addition to helping you with your specific goals, you may find yourself very relaxed and in a great mood after your sessions. This is because hypnosis is a relaxing and natural stress reducer. How's that for a nice side effect?

The Instant Self-Hypnosis Reader's Induction

(to be read aloud)

"Feeling a sense of privacy and comfort, I allow the sound of my own voice to soothe my mind and body while I speak slowly and softly. My body is slowing *down* as though everything is moving in slow motion. With every word I read and every sound I utter, I feel *more relaxed* and at peace. Moment by moment, my mind is becoming as *clear* as the surface of a calm and quiet mountain lake.

"As my mind clears, I use my imagination to *relax more deeply* while I read. I imagine that I am sitting on a comfortable chair on a beautiful beach. With my peripheral vision, I see the golden sand that surrounds me...and the waves crashing on the shore. I hear the gentle and rhythmic sounds they make.

"I feel a moist sea breeze waft over my body. I notice the warm sun on my skin. I feel its golden touch on my scalp, allowing me to let go of any excess tension in my scalp. All of my thoughts seem to *quiet down now* as I concentrate my attention on the sun's warmth on my face...on my cheeks...on my ears...and around my jaw.

"The healing light seems to caress my neck and to warm my throat, allowing the words to flow easily and effortlessly from my mouth. It feels as though hundreds of tiny fingers of light are massaging my shoulders and my upper back as I relax—waves of warmth and relaxation cascade down...down my arms and out through my fingers.

"As I take a slow breath and exhale I become aware of this relaxing feeling filling my chest (take a breath and exhale slowly). A golden-yellow radiance floods my solar plexus as I take another slow breath and *release* it (take another breath)…and I feel sense of tranquility and *deep peacefulness* fill my entire stomach area.

"I mentally scan my hips, pelvis, and buttocks…and let any tension or anxiety there be gently washed away by a stream of light. I become aware of my legs now…they are almost aglow as sunlight floods down through them. My legs feel so relaxed. Even my feet and toes feel warm and comfortable…warm and comfortable now.

"As I bask in the glorious sun, I imagine closing my eyes as I prepare to hypnotize myself. I draw three slow deep breaths (draw three deep breaths). For a few moments I can see the glow of orange light through my closed eyelids. But now that light fades into a comforting darkness as I draw my attention inward…*inward*…toward the *center* of my mind.

"I imagine that I am approaching a tall, modern, and familiar building. I walk through the revolving door and step into a beautiful lobby. Inside the building stands a strong, armed security guard who secures the building from intruders. The guard looks at me with a steely glare, but then recognizes me as the owner of the building. The guard works for me. I give the guard a self-satisfied nod and make my way toward the elevator.

"I see the reflection of myself in the mirrorlike surface of the elevator doors. I look relaxed and confident. I press the down arrow and the doors of the elevator open. *I feel very safe* as I step into a spacious and luxurious elevator car. I turn toward the panel of buttons which indicate the floor numbers. I press the number ten, which lights up as the elevator doors close. The elevator car begins to move down smoothly through the long, deep elevator shaft…with a very gentle humming sound. I watch the numbered lights above the door as they change. Each number lights up for a moment as the elevator moves past the indicated floor. As the numbers change…one by one…I feel myself descending to a wonderful place within myself…far beneath the surface.

"One…I watch the numbers as the elevator moves down…deeper down with every number.

"Two…deeper beneath the surface of this great structure…down below the surface now.

"Three…by the time I reach the tenth number, I will be hypnotized.

"Four…I will be hypnotized with my eyes open…open to all beneficial suggestions.

"Five…I feel myself descending…smoothly…effortlessly.

"Six…still watching the number change above the door…one by one.

"Seven…going deeper now…feeling peaceful and relaxed.

"Eight…I am safe…I feel calm…going down…down…deeper down.

"Nine…I allow myself to enter into hypnosis with my eyes open.

"Ten…the elevator car comes to a smooth halt as I reach my destination.

"As the doors open, I enter into a comfortably furnished reading room. A burning log in the fireplace crackles and blazes brightly, as if welcoming me into the chamber. I approach a very comfortable-looking chair and sit down. I pick up a book on a small table next to the chair. I read the cover of the book, which says *Instant Self-Hypnosis*. I open the book and begin to read. And the words address me directly and seem to jump off of the pages and into my mind. Here is what they say:

"'You are now hypnotized with your eyes open. You are now highly suggestible. You will remain in hypnosis while you read the suggestions for your goal. Your mind soaks in the suggestions now the way a sponge soaks in water. You can easily *stay hypnotized* with your eyes open until you read the 'Wake-Up.' You remain *calm and focused* as you turn to your bookmark.'"

(Please turn to your selected script.)

Stop Stressing Out

The following suggestions are designed to reduce or eliminate general feelings of anxiety and nervous tension.

"I now eliminate anxious or nervous feelings throughout the day.

"I *feel relaxed* and comfortable throughout every day, just as I feel right now. I *let go* of tension and tightness and release forever anxious feelings in my body and mind. Throughout the day, I will now become very aware any time I hold excess muscular tension in my body. And when I become aware of it, I will take a deep breath. As I then release the breath, I will also relax the tensed area. As my body relaxes, I immediately *feel better*. By letting go of tension, I let go of feelings of anxiety…because it's very difficult to feel nervous or tense when my body is relaxed.

"From now on I feel relaxed and focused when dealing with my work. I have a pleasant attitude throughout my day…and find life more joyful. I *feel totally comfortable* when dealing with people and my relationships. My body is becoming healthier now that I utilize its energy resources in a wiser manner. *I feel more optimistic* about my plans because feelings of anxiety are evaporating like drops of water on a hot, sunny day. I take the time to enjoy the people, places, and events of my daily life.

"I imagine feeling totally relaxed as I wake up to begin a new day. I picture myself stretching and yawning with a sense of deep peace and optimism. Feeling refreshed, I realize how good it feels to be free of anxiety and just look forward to each part of my day. As I make my way to the bathroom and begin cleansing and grooming my body, an inner feeling of cleansing is taking place in my body and my emotions. Things inside me feel clean and orderly, and I know I can choose to continue *feeling relaxed, focused, and positive* throughout my day. There is an underlying sense of peace and safety within me that permeates every part of my body and my thoughts. Worry and anxiety have been washed away, down the drain…and in their place I feel happy and relaxed, comfortable and tranquil as I go about my day.

"From now on, I choose to feel relaxed and free of anxiety. Whenever I start to observe any feelings of anxiety, all I have to do is clench my fist and release it as I count slowly to three. When I reach the number three and as I totally release the tension from my fist, the anxiety will be gone and I will feel comfortable and relaxed."

(The Wake-Up)

"I will awaken from hypnosis by counting to five. When I reach the number five, I will become fully alert and wide awake. One…beginning to awaken from hypnosis. Two…becoming aware of my surroundings…feeling satisfied, safe, and comfortable. Three…looking forward to positive results from this hypnosis session. Four…feeling absolutely wonderful. FIVE…FIVE…FIVE…now wide awake and fully alert."

More Fun at Parties

The following suggestions are designed to increase assertiveness in social settings only. They are to help you to feel comfortable with starting and holding casual conversations, relaxing, and having a good time.

"I now *have more fun* in social settings.

"From now on, I *have a good time* at parties and I participate in conversation and festivities with ease. I allow myself to enjoy social situations. I let go of nervousness and tension and *have more fun* during activities with friends and loved ones. I am *more self-assertive* in all social activities…whether with friends, business associates, or strangers.

"I easily engage in small talk with people in social settings while feeling relaxed and comfortable. I act *like myself.* I speak my opinions and enjoy sharing my views, letting my words *flow naturally*…effortlessly. I introduce myself to strangers at social functions and initiate conversation. I take great interest in group conversations and listen to what others have to say. I then assert my own opinions, knowing that my views are insightful and valuable.

"I have much to offer in social situations. My presence is valuable. My participation is appreciated. I know that people like me. I can be myself at all times. I choose from now on to participate in conversation or in festivities I enjoy. Whether *I want to laugh,* or *dance,* or choose to *participate in fun* and games…I naturally show my wonderful *personality* and permit others to enjoy my presence.

"I imagine enjoying myself at a party with friends and strangers. I picture myself laughing as someone says something funny. It makes *me think of something funny*…and I share it with others. I enjoy what I am saying and I enjoy sharing.

"My body language is relaxed and confident, as a conversation turns to a more serious topic. I hear myself sharing my knowledge and offering my opinions…and I watch those around me nod their heads with acknowledgment and agreement. As the words flow freely from my mouth, I realize that *I am intelligent* and that others see me that way.

"I *enjoy mingling*.…At the party, and I find myself walking up to a perfect stranger and introducing myself with a confident smile. The stranger returns the smile and appreciates that I am so assertive as I begin conversation. *I feel free*…just realizing how easy it is to relax and be myself at this party. I have so much fun that I look forward to attending parties and social functions in the future.

"From now on, I look forward to attending social functions. I have a strong desire to join in conversations and assert my opinions. My voice, as I speak, sounds clear and confident. From now on, when a man or woman engages me in conversation, I will recognize that my words have great value both to me and to the listener. So I will automatically relax and feel at ease…just as I feel right now…during conversation with friends, with business associates, and even with strangers. When the festivities include activities such as dancing or games, I will decide whether the activity is something I honestly enjoy or want to enjoy. If it is something to enjoy, I will assert myself, join in the activity, and enjoy myself totally. It feels so good to let go and have fun. I am a fun person. I let go and have fun. More fun now."

(The Wake-Up)

"I will awaken from hypnosis by counting to five. When I reach the number five, I will become fully alert and wide awake. One…beginning to awaken from hypnosis. Two…becoming aware of my surroundings…feeling satisfied, safe, and comfortable. Three…looking forward to positive results from this hypnosis session. Four…feeling absolutely wonderful. FIVE…FIVE…FIVE…now wide awake and fully alert."

Super-Assertive in Business

The following suggestions are designed
to increase assertiveness in the workplace,
business settings, and attaining career success.

"I am *super assertive* and confident in my job and career.

"I now assert myself in all business situations. I *want to achieve* recognition for my work and *get credit* for my ideas. I choose to share my good ideas and offer input to my supervisor, coworkers, and business associates. I *now seek* greater success in the *work I want* to do. I do my job confidently and efficiently and produce creative solutions to any problem in my work.

"I communicate my professional opinions with confidence and eloquence. I apply myself to do the best possible work. I calmly stand up for myself when challenged by supervisors or coworkers. I *feel enthusiastic* and proud of the work I do and let others recognize my abilities. I enjoy business meetings and seize opportunities to speak my mind when I have something to say. I *feel courageous* at the workplace and *credit myself* for my abilities and intelligence. I can handle any business crisis calmly, quickly, and intelligently. I feel valued by my peers. What I do is important. I am important. I will achieve success and apply myself toward promotions. I can achieve more success. I want to succeed. I deserve *success now* in my career. I believe in myself and my abilities.

"I can imagine myself sitting with confidence at a conference table now, amid several other business associates. I see myself being attentive to the business conversation. I know that my *input is vital* to success, so I offer to *share* my business ideas and I take initiative in all business situations. As the meeting comes to a close, I see myself walking up to the most influential businessperson there and speaking with great confidence about my work and ideas. My ideas are received with great enthusiasm, and the green light is given for me to implement my plans. And as I walk out of the conference room, I feel a great sense of accomplishment…knowing that when I assert myself, I *advance my career* and success. I see myself doing what I know how to do as I *take great pride* in my work. I hear others give me compliments on how good I am at what I do. I am *enjoying my work* in a whole new way.

"From now on, I *assert myself* in all business situations. I feel relaxed and confident when sharing my ideas with business people. Whenever I *assert my ideas* and share my professional knowledge with others, my voice is clear and confident. I am nobody's doormat. When challenged by anyone in business or at the workplace, I will stand up for my actions and my views, calmly and rationally. Day by day, I am *more assertive* in my career. Ideas on how to improve my job performance or advance my career come to mind easily and quickly. I am *totally self-assured* in my professional knowledge and expertise. From now on, I give myself credit for a job well done. I am now *more successful.* I want to…and deserve to…succeed in any business-related activity.

"I am determined to succeed in my career and I *focus my priorities* on it. I *feel the determination* filling me even now. The determination feels very strong and very liberating…and I know that nothing can stop me. I trust myself. I trust my ideas. I am positive that *I will succeed.*"

(The Wake-Up)

"I will awaken from hypnosis by counting to five. When I reach the number five, I will become fully alert and wide awake. One…beginning to awaken from hypnosis. Two…becoming aware of my surroundings…feeling satisfied, safe, and comfortable. Three…looking forward to positive results from this hypnosis session. Four…feeling absolutely wonderful. FIVE…FIVE…FIVE…now wide awake and fully alert."

Success

This script is designed to eliminate the fear of failure
and to encourage a proactive stance in goal manifestation.
You should already have a specific goal in mind to
use this script for optimal results.

"I *will* and I *want* to succeed with my goal, whether personal or professional.

"I have the heart of a *lion*. I have the wings of an *eagle*. I have the wisdom of an *angel*. I have the determination of a *bull*. I can and *I will succeed* in whatever I put my mind to, and I won't stop no matter who or what appears to get in my way. For I am motivated to succeed. I am designed for success. And I know that success is achievable.

"There is no such thing as failure. There are only results. But I must seek to find. I must knock to have the doors open. So I take action. And when a result is not what I am looking for, I examine the result…I learn from the result, and then I try again. And again. And again.

"I imagine that my goal is like a target. And I am an archer. I am becoming an expert marksman. I know my target. I learn how to shoot an arrow. And I aim for the bullseye. Even if I don't hit the bullseye the first time, even if I don't hit the target at all…that's okay. There are only results. I can take another shot. I can shoot another arrow. And I keep taking aim…and I keep releasing arrows until I hit the bull's eye…until I am satisfied. With every arrow I release, my conscious and my subconscious minds now work together to readjust and recalculate in order to hit the bullseye…to accomplish my goal…to succeed.

"I know what I want. I will go after it. I dare to put my mind, my emotions, and my body to work for what I want. And I now call upon all allied forces, people, institutions to aid me in my quest. The universe and life itself are on my side. I am supported above and below, to the left and to the right, ahead of me and behind me, from within me and beyond me.

"I keep silent about my goal. I tell no one except those who will directly assist me in achieving it. I remain quiet about my goal even with friends and family unless absolutely necessary. I do this to concentrate my inner fire, my concentration to succeed. I don't need everyone's comments or suggestions because I know what I want, and I believe I can do it, have it, achieve it. So I keep silent about my goal as much as possible until *I've attained it.* I only inform those who will directly assist me.

"Nothing happens unless I make it happen. *Success will come* to me as I go toward it. So I *take the next step* toward my ultimate goal. After this session, I will think about the next step. What is it? What is the very next thing I can do to get closer to my goal? I picture and imagine myself taking the next step." (Take a moment now and picture it…even with your eyes open.)

(The Wake-Up)

"I will awaken from hypnosis by counting to five. When I reach the number five, I will become fully alert and wide awake. One…beginning to awaken from hypnosis. Two…becoming aware of my surroundings…feeling satisfied, safe, and comfortable. Three…looking forward to positive results from this hypnosis session. Four…feeling absolutely wonderful. FIVE…FIVE…FIVE…now wide awake and fully alert."

Public Speaking

The following suggestions are designed to
eliminate the fear of public speaking

"I feel relaxed and confident when speaking to a group of people.

"Whenever I get up to speak, I will draw one slow, deep breath. And as I release it slowly, all tension and anxiety I feel about speaking in front of others will also be released. I will discover *I feel fine*. I will *feel at ease* as I begin to talk. It will feel almost as though I am talking to a friend about a subject I know very well.

"I *prepare thoroughly* for my speaking engagements. I know my subject very well, so talking about it will be *easy and natural* no matter who or how many people I am speaking to. The truth is that I will probably know more about my subject than the people to whom I will be speaking. So I have nothing to feel nervous about. Instead, I will *feel deeply absorbed* in what I am saying, forgetting about everything else.

"The people I speak to are my equals. So I no longer want or need to feel self-conscious in any way when I speak in public. I will *feel confident and relaxed* as I speak. I will focus on what I am saying without feeling nervous or embarrassed. I realize that people want to hear the knowledge and information I possess. My *mind stays sharp* and clear as I discuss the points I want to make.

"As I begin to speak, I realize it doesn't matter how many people are looking at and listening to me. The information remains the same. I am able to deliver information in a relaxed and pleasant tone of voice. I *feel fine* whether in front of one person, a few people, or many people. It's all the same to me from now on. I feel fine in front of any number of people.

"I will remember that no matter who is in the audience or how important they may seem to be, they are really just people...who eat, sleep, and use the toilet...just like everybody else.

"When I speak in front of an audience, I will feel perfectly at ease. Even as I think about speaking to a group now, *I feel just fine.* And I will continue to *feel just fine* whenever I get up to speak before others.

"When I get up to speak, I will draw a slow, deep breath. As I let it out, I will let go of any anxiety I feel. And on the next breath I will discover that *I feel great. I feel ready* to give the audience the information I have prepared for them. I feel fine as I speak to the audience."

(The Wake-Up)

"I will awaken from hypnosis by counting to five. When I reach the number five, I will become fully alert and wide awake. One...beginning to awaken from hypnosis. Two...becoming aware of my surroundings...feeling satisfied, safe, and comfortable. Three...looking forward to positive results from this hypnosis session. Four...feeling absolutely wonderful. FIVE...FIVE...FIVE...now wide awake and fully alert."

Eliminate Allergies

The following suggestions are designed to reduce or eliminate allergic reaction to a specific airborne substance (e.g. pollen). Important: do not use this script for food allergies.

Special Instructions: Choose one airborne allergen to work on per session. Wherever you see a blank space in the script, say the name of the allergen.

"I free myself from any allergic reaction to _____.

"Day by day, I am gaining more freedom from any allergy to _____. I now let go of worry and preoccupation with the presence of _____ in the air. I will become less aware of the presence of _____, and forget that I ever had the allergy. I will be able to *breathe fresh air* indoors and outdoors letting my lungs take in oxygen and fill my body with energy. I will let go of coughing, sneezing, wheezing and all other reactions I once had to _____.

"I will be able to breathe freely in the presence of _____. I will be able to focus deeply on whatever I am doing so that I am no longer preoccupied or concerned with _____. I will feel relaxed, confident, and happy as I *become free* from any allergic response to _____. The tension in my body will decrease as I feel completely at ease around the presence of _____. I will have a sense of emotional and physical well-being even when I am around _____.

"I imagine myself at home, in bed, waking up on a weekend morning. The sun shines outside the window and I take a deep, rousing breath, filling my lungs with air. The breath both relaxes and invigorates me, so I take in deep breaths of healthy air. My breathing is free and easy. I feel myself *breathing effortlessly* through my nose…and can smell the sweet, fragrant air coming through an open window. I had the window open all night and slept perfectly through the night…breathing perfectly, healthfully, unobstructed breaths. As I visualize myself beginning my day, I go outside and continue feeling totally relaxed. I am enjoying outside activities, confidently and safely. At night, I attend a small gathering of friends at someone else's home. I relax and am not even aware of whether _____ is in the air.

"I now instruct my immune system to reduce and correct its overreaction to _____. Day by day, my allergy to _____ is disappearing and I *am breathing more comfortably* and easily."

(The Wake-Up)

"I will awaken from hypnosis by counting to five. When I reach the number five, I will become fully alert and wide awake. One…beginning to awaken from hypnosis. Two…becoming aware of my surroundings…feeling satisfied, safe, and comfortable. Three…looking forward to positive results from this hypnosis session. Four…feeling absolutely wonderful. FIVE…FIVE…FIVE…now wide awake and fully alert."

Stop Teeth Grinding

The following suggestions are designed to stop the
grinding of teeth both at night and during the daytime.

"I now stop grinding my teeth.

"I stop myself from grinding my teeth both at night and in the day-time. I am aware whenever I start grinding my teeth…and I immediately *relax my jaw* and my mouth. I find other ways to *relieve tension* and stress so that I can *now stop grinding* my teeth and clenching my jaw. At night, as I sleep, I let every part of my body relax…including my jaw and my mouth. In the day, I handle any situation calmly and efficiently…without grinding my teeth. I stop eating myself up with stress, as I *now stop grinding* my teeth.

"I have healthier teeth as I learn to *stop myself* from grinding my teeth. I *feel better* and relieve tension in more productive ways. I have *more productive sleep* and feel more rested in the morning once I discontinue grinding my teeth. My dentist will be *more pleased* with me when I *stop grinding* my teeth. I prevent dental problems as I *stop* grinding my teeth. I get more in touch with subconscious sources of stress and find better ways to *relieve my tension*. I feel more self-confident, knowing that I can teach myself to stop teeth grinding. I am more in control of my behaviors, both conscious and subconscious.

"I imagine myself during a stressful part of my day. I *become aware* that I am holding a lot of stress in my jaw…that I am holding my jaw so tight and grinding my teeth. As I become aware of what I am doing, I smile and *release the tension* in my mouth. I notice how much *better I feel* as I relax my jaw. At night, as I go to sleep, I picture myself closing my eyes and feeling my jaw and mouth letting go of tension and stress…as I slip into a *restful slumber.* My jaw *remains relaxed* the whole night, and I wake up refreshed in every part of my body.

"From now on, I will become aware any time I am grinding my teeth or clenching my jaw. As I become aware, I will immediately relax my mouth and feel a sense of calm. Day by day, I form a new behavior…a healthy habit of relaxing my jaw and mouth. In a very short time, keeping my jaw relaxed becomes natural to me…and I will no longer grind my teeth at all. Instead, I will choose to relax…let go of stress in my body. I know I can relax, just as I am doing right now, without grinding my teeth."

(The Wake-Up)

"I will awaken from hypnosis by counting to five. When I reach the number five, I will become fully alert and wide awake. One…beginning to awaken from hypnosis. Two…becoming aware of my surroundings…feeling satisfied, safe, and comfortable. Three…looking forward to positive results from this hypnosis session. Four…feeling absolutely wonderful. FIVE…FIVE…FIVE…now wide awake and fully alert."

Perfect Concentration

The following suggestions are designed
to increase general concentration.

"I have excellent concentration with everything I do.

"From now on, I *concentrate* on a task…and give it my full attention. I *focus* on what I am doing with great intensity. Details are very interesting, and my attention will remain fixed on the task at hand. Perfect mental clarity is mine…as my *concentration now* increases. As a result of better concentration, I retain more information and perform each task with great efficiency. I *narrow my focus* on whatever I am doing with perfect concentration…perfect concentration on what I choose to do.

"My mind remains fixed on my current task without wandering. I can focus completely…free of worry, anxiety, or restlessness. I am able to *concentrate easily* because it is natural for me to do so. I take pleasure in each task or activity as my concentration increases…because I find that I am fascinated by that on which *I focus my attention*. I shift my total concentration to any subject or any activity with great ease and mental agility. My body and mind work together to give me *total concentration*.

"Right now, I imagine myself reading a book. It is a textbook designed to impart important information to me. My total fixed attention is on the words of this book. I find the information interesting, and my ability to concentrate and absorb the information is very high. The more I read, the more interesting I find the book. The details of the book are fascinating to me, and I find that my mind absorbs the information readily. As I read, my body is in a perfect position to accompany my sense of perfect concentration. My posture is good. My breathing is steady and rhythmic. As I turn the pages of the book, I find that I *can stay perfectly focused* on what I am reading…and that minor disturbances around me no longer bother me. I can continue to read and *concentrate perfectly* until I decide I wish to stop.

"From now on, my concentration on a task will increase. I associate my ability to concentrate on any task with my obvious ability to concentrate while I read this script. I have total concentration on what I am doing now…so whatever else I choose to pay attention to, I will have the same amount of total fixed attention. And I can *remain focused* until the task is finished or until I choose to turn my *total attention* to something else. I have perfect concentration."

(The Wake-Up)

"I will awaken from hypnosis by counting to five. When I reach the number five, I will become fully alert and wide awake. One…beginning to awaken from hypnosis. Two…becoming aware of my surroundings…feeling satisfied, safe, and comfortable. Three…looking forward to positive results from this hypnosis session. Four…feeling absolutely wonderful. FIVE…FIVE…FIVE…now wide awake and fully alert."

Amazing Dream Recall

The following suggestions are designed to
promote retention of dreams upon awakening.

"I remember my dreams when I wake up in the morning.

"My memory of my dreams and all of the details gets better and bet-ter every day. Upon awakening, I'm able to recall the images, sounds, and feelings I experienced in my dreams. I can do this very easily and effortlessly. I retain…in vivid detail…the events as they appeared in my dreams.

"I value the ability of my subconscious mind to create dreams for me. I am strengthening the communication between my conscious and subconscious minds right now through the tool of hypnosis. And I use hypnosis as a means to instruct my subconscious to allow *perfect recall* of my dreams upon awakening. My mind records and remembers dreams that are important for me to recall.

"I feel a sense of satisfaction that I am able *to recount the images* and events from my dreams. I am able to *recall dreams* and write down all details with *total clarity* if I choose. By remembering my dreams, I will *gain insights* to my life in order to live better and *be more productive*.

"I imagine waking up in the morning now, after a restful night's sleep. As I lay in bed, I remain quiet and allow my mind to *recall the details* of an important dream I had while asleep. I picture myself remembering the dream so vividly…that it's like experiencing it all over again, even while I am awake. The *details are vivid* and bright, and the events are fresh in my mind. I reach for a notepad or journal next to the bed and I write down the dream I had with perfect clarity. I can remember exactly how the dream began, how it ended…and all of the details of the dream in between. First this, then that, and so on…until I have recalled the entire dream.

"From now on, when I wake up, the memory of dreams from the night instantly surface in my mind…swiftly and with ease and clarity.

"Tomorrow morning when I awaken naturally from sleep, I will pause for a minute before getting out of bed. And as I relax for a minute, the memory of the night's dreams will become fully active. I will remember the night's dreams with complete ease. I will let the *vivid details* of the dreams rise to the surface of my awareness. I will have total and amazing recall of my dreams."

(The Wake-Up)

"I will awaken from hypnosis by counting to five. When I reach the number five, I will become fully alert and wide awake. One…beginning to awaken from hypnosis. Two…becoming aware of my surroundings…feeling satisfied, safe, and comfortable. Three…looking forward to positive results from this hypnosis session. Four…feeling absolutely wonderful. FIVE…FIVE…FIVE…now wide awake and fully alert."

Lucid Dreams Tonight

The following suggestions are designed to encourage
dreams in which one becomes self-aware.

"I become aware that I am dreaming while I continue to dream.

"I am now able to realize while asleep that I am in the midst of a dream. I am aware when I am dreaming, and I control my own actions. I *have lucid dreams*, without waking up from sleep. I will realize that I am actually asleep in bed but that I am still asleep as I dream. I will become a *self-aware observer* as well as a participant of my dreams.

"When I *become aware* that I am dreaming, I have more control over my dreams. I am able to effect the outcome of my dreams as I become self-aware while dreaming. I will have more fun while I sleep as I *become lucid while dreaming*.

"I imagine myself in bed asleep at night. From somewhere deep inside my mind…images, sounds, and feelings are conjured, as my mind's inner movie projector presents a dream. Suddenly, in a flash of insight, I feel myself become aware that the images are a projection of my mind…I realize that I am in the middle of a dream. I am completely aware that what I see, hear, and feel is a product of my own mind. I also realize that I can say or do anything I wish to say or do in the dream as the dream continues. I can even choose to change the images and events in the dream by gently and confidently using my will power.

"I am a *lucid dreamer now*. I experience lucid dreams. Beginning tonight, I will produce a dream in which I become self-aware. I will know that I am dreaming and that I have full control over my actions in the dream. I will remember the lucid dreams that I have so that I can enjoy thinking about them the next day.

"I am a lucid dreamer. I have lucid dreams when I sleep."

(The Wake-Up)

"I will awaken from hypnosis by counting to five. When I reach the number five, I will become fully alert and wide awake. One...beginning to awaken from hypnosis. Two...becoming aware of my surroundings...feeling satisfied, safe, and comfortable. Three...looking forward to positive results from this hypnosis session. Four...feeling absolutely wonderful. FIVE...FIVE...FIVE...now wide awake and fully alert."

Bye-Bye Bad Habit

The following suggestions are designed to eliminate
an unwanted behavioral habit and replace it with
feelings of relaxation and well-being.

Special Instructions: Choose one habit to work on
per session. Wherever you see a blank space in
the script, say the name of the habit.

"I now stop the behavior of _____.

"I now gain control over my desire to _____. I now let go of
my need or desire to _____…and I'll choose freedom instead. I
forgive myself for my behavior, and I give myself permission and
encouragement to stop myself from _____.

"My behavior of _____ is just a pattern of behavior. The habit
is based on thoughts…and *thoughts change*. It's a pattern that my mind
has been repeating. With the power of my subconscious mind through
hypnosis, I interrupt and *change that pattern* now. I will find that I am
losing the desire to _____ on a subconscious level. I am replacing the desire to hold on to that behavior with a habit of feeling
relaxed, happy, and free of the habit to _____ now.

"I let go of guilt or shame over my behavior of _____ because
guilt and shame are a waste of time. I now see that, day by day, I am
gaining more control over myself and my behavior. I will no longer
_____ by habit. I will *become hyperaware* each time I begin to
_____. When I *become hyperaware*, I will take a deep breath and
relax…and then I'll realize that I have free will and can simply choose

to do something other than _____. Each time I choose not to _____, I will feel a sense of control and confidence. I prefer the feeling of being self-controlled and relaxed to what I feel when I _____. I am losing my interest in _____. As I give it less of my interest, I find that I _____ less and less.

"It's much easier now to stop myself from _____ than I ever imagined. I realize now that I have more control over my mind and my body than I gave myself credit for. And now that I've clearly asked and instructed my subconscious mind to assist me to stop myself from _____, success will come quickly and easily. A habit is based on a thought. A thought can be changed. I choose to change the thought and release emotional attachment to _____. I am a strong, attractive, capable individual. I can handle any of life's problems without the need to _____. It never really helped me to begin with, and now I release it from my life and choose to feel secure, confident, and happy just being me."

(The Wake-Up)

"I will awaken from hypnosis by counting to five. When I reach the number five, I will become fully alert and wide awake. One…beginning to awaken from hypnosis. Two…becoming aware of my surroundings…feeling satisfied, safe, and comfortable. Three…looking forward to positive results from this hypnosis session. Four…feeling absolutely wonderful. FIVE…FIVE…FIVE…now wide awake and fully alert."

Feeling Dandy at the Dentist

The following suggestions are designed to
reduce or eliminate fear of going to the dentist
and when undergoing dental procedures.

"I feel relaxed and comfortable about making dental appointments, and I release my fear of dental procedures.

"I want my teeth and mouth to be healthy to avoid problems and pain in the future. The dentist helps me obtain that goal. So I will *feel relaxed* and comfortable visiting the dentist and sitting in the dental chair. My muscles will relax…and my jaw will become *loose and comfortable* as I allow the dental treatment…knowing that I want healthy teeth and gums. I will allow my dentist to help me become more healthy, so I remain relaxed and cooperative. I let go of anxiety and feel great about setting and keeping dental appointments.

"I *feel at ease* as I walk in the door of the dentist. I feel great about having made an appointment to go see the dentist. I know my health will improve as I see the dentist, as fear and apprehension *fade away* now. I am able to let the dentist work on my teeth and perform the procedures that are needed for my own well-being. My mouth *no longer tenses* up. My jaw will *become loose and agile* so that the dentist is pleased with my total cooperation.

"I picture myself picking up the phone to make an appointment for the dentist. The receptionist is kind as the appointment is secured, and I feel better already about making the appointment. I imagine days pass…and now I am walking through the door to the dentist's office. As I pass through the door, I feel cool…calm…and relaxed. As

I am brought to the dental chair, I am at *complete ease*. I consider the appointment a nice break from the rest of my day. And as the dentist begins working with me, my jaw stays nice and relaxed, *free of tension*. The dental tools...I see them and hear them, but I now realize they are just helpful instruments to assist in my dental health, so I *feel just fine* about them.

"From now on, I become more relaxed whenever I enter the doorway of the dentist's office. When I sit in the dental chair, I notice how relaxed the design of the chair makes me feel. I let my body relax and feel completely comfortable. When I see and hear dental tools, I find them interesting...but I continue to stay calm and at ease. I look forward to my time in the dental chair, using it as a nice break in my busy day."

(The Wake-Up)

"I will awaken from hypnosis by counting to five. When I reach the number five, I will become fully alert and wide awake. One...beginning to awaken from hypnosis. Two...becoming aware of my surroundings...feeling satisfied, safe, and comfortable. Three...looking forward to positive results from this hypnosis session. Four...feeling absolutely wonderful. FIVE...FIVE...FIVE...now wide awake and fully alert."

Become More Decisive and Efficient

The following suggestions are designed to increase decisiveness and efficiency in performing tasks and confidence in decision making.

"I now become more decisive and increase my efficiency."

"I now increase my ability to make decisions and stick to them. I stop doubting and accept my ability to *make good decisions. I feel confident* in taking *decisive action* in any task. I will be *more efficient* by prioritizing and organizing my tasks for the day. I *decide easily* what needs to be done and in what order things need to get done. I no longer second guess my decisions. I trust myself. I will *choose* a course of *action* and stick with it.

"I *feel relaxed* about my decisions…and I carry them out with ease and grace. When distractions occur, I deal with them quickly…and then I return to my decided course of activity. I allow myself to select the optimum choice after considering the pros and cons of each alternative. I believe that my choice is correct and *the best choice* I can make with the time that I have. I gracefully go about a group of tasks, organizing them and carefully prioritizing them with *total competence* and confidence. I choose what needs to be done and in what order and then begin completing each task until I am finished with it for the day. I *remain focused* on a task until I have completed it to my satisfaction. I decide to stop myself from questioning my ability to *make good decisions.* I let go of distractions and disorganization now and focus on what I want to get done…focus on my priorities.

"I imagine now that I am sitting at a desk with many papers and tasks in front of me. I prioritize what needs to be done and organize the papers carefully and easily. I decide to begin working with the most important task and save the others for later. I imagine there is a phone on my desk and it rings. I answer it politely…and immediately let the caller know that I am busy and that I will return their call when I am finished with my current task. As I hang up the phone, my mind returns to the task in front of me, and I picture myself working with focus and determination. As I finish the first task, I feel great about myself…and even afford myself a short break. I return the phone call I received but talk only for a few minutes. After the break, my mind is refreshed and I begin decisively working on the next task.

"From now on, I trust my ability to *make a decision.* I am becoming very decisive. I choose among my options and *follow through* with my plans. I am becoming proficient with all tasks. I am becoming more efficient each day by *organizing and prioritizing* both small and large tasks."

(The Wake-Up)

"I will awaken from hypnosis by counting to five. When I reach the number five, I will become fully alert and wide awake. One…beginning to awaken from hypnosis. Two…becoming aware of my surroundings…feeling satisfied, safe, and comfortable. Three…looking forward to positive results from this hypnosis session. Four…feeling absolutely wonderful. FIVE…FIVE…FIVE…now wide awake and fully alert."

More Energy Now

The following suggestions are designed to reduce fatigue and increase physical energy as well as enthusiasm in daily life.

"I have more energy and enthusiasm in everything that I do.

"I enjoy each aspect of my life more…as my energy and enthusiasm increases greatly day by day. I am able to *feel more alive* and become more excited now about whatever I do. I want to live life to the fullest and *get more satisfaction* from every activity. Having *more energy now* will help me to do this. I have more fun when I *feel more energy*. I choose to feel more healthy and vibrant as my energy increases. My sense of vitality dramatically increases now as I become excited and enthusiastic about my life.

"I let go of feelings of fatigue and apathy now…so that I can involve myself with new endeavors with zeal and fervor. I let my happy, energetic side emerge…so that others can enjoy my personality and presence. I feel energetic when I wake up in the morning. I will have more energy throughout my day. I enjoy the vital sensations of my body and of being more mentally alert. I am now able to do the things I really want to do with sustained energy, interest, and enthusiasm. My mood is now brighter…my disposition is sunny…as I become more energetic.

"I imagine that at night, while I sleep, my *body recharges* like a battery…so that when I awaken from a good night's sleep, my battery is totally recharged…full of energy. I wake up in the morning and I *feel revitalized*…as though my body is full of yellow light or sunshine. This makes me feel so good and totally alive. As I get up and take a shower, the sensation of the water against my body makes me feel wonderful and energetic…and I feel excited about what my day will bring. As I get dressed, I imagine putting on clothes that match my *happy mood.* I picture myself eating healthy foods for breakfast and drinking plenty of fresh water. As I walk out the door, I realize that *I am smiling*…and that I feel enthusiastic and energetic…and that this feeling will stay with me the rest of the day!

"Each day I wake up, I will have more energy than the day that came before. I let go of my desire to feel fatigue and apathy…and am replacing it with a *fresh desire* to feel cheerful and energetic. I desire to appreciate myself as a vigorous, energetic human being. I am alive!"

(The Wake-Up)

"I will awaken from hypnosis by counting to five. When I reach the number five, I will become fully alert and wide awake. One…beginning to awaken from hypnosis. Two…becoming aware of my surroundings…feeling satisfied, safe, and comfortable. Three…looking forward to positive results from this hypnosis session. Four…feeling absolutely wonderful. FIVE…FIVE…FIVE…now wide awake and fully alert."

Fly without Fear

The following suggestions are designed to
reduce stress and anxiety when on an airplane.

"I feel relaxed and comfortable while traveling by airplane or jet.

"I feel absolutely fine about making reservations for a flight. I look forward to getting aboard the plane, feeling relaxed and at peace with myself. When I sit down in my assigned seat, I let my body *completely relax* and I can breathe deeply and freely. As the doors of the plane close, I choose to *feel secure* and safe. I will remember that flying is statistically safer than driving a car…that I am *safer on a plane* than in a car.

"I am able to board a plane to carry me where I want to go…faster and easier than other modes of transportation. When I choose to travel by plane, I *let go of anxiety* about my travel plans—and I remember that flying reduces travel time. I *feel more confident* in myself, as I realize how much control I have over my feelings. I am able to make reservations for a flight without hesitation when I release the fear of flying now. I can enjoy the flight…as I decide to *relax and feel secure now* about flying.

"I imagine calling the airline and making a reservation. My voice is clear and confident. I *feel good* about making the reservations…knowing that for long distances, flying is the safest and most logical choice of transportation.

"Time passes and the day of the flight arrives. I get my ticket and hear the loudspeaker announce that my plane is now boarding. As I get on the plane and the flight attendant greets me, I realize that the flight attendant is a professional and that she has flown safely hundreds of times. As I find my way to my seat and *feel the comfortable cushion* underneath me, I relax my body and draw a deep breath. As I release my breath slowly, my emotions become calm and level. As the doors are closed, I recognize the plane is being secured for my safety. When I hear the sound of the captain's voice over the speaker, I picture him in uniform and recognize that he has professional training...and experience in *safe flying*. And as the plane takes off, I discover that I feel relaxed and secure...that everything is going to be fine.

"From now on, I feel more relaxed about flying on planes. When I sip the beverage of my choice during the flight, each sip will relax me more and more. I will let go of the desire to worry, and I will allow myself to enjoy the flight."

(The Wake-Up)

"I will awaken from hypnosis by counting to five. When I reach the number five, I will become fully alert and wide awake. One...beginning to awaken from hypnosis. Two...becoming aware of my surroundings...feeling satisfied, safe, and comfortable. Three...looking forward to positive results from this hypnosis session. Four...feeling absolutely wonderful. FIVE...FIVE...FIVE...now wide awake and fully alert."

End Fingernail Biting

The following suggestions are designed
to eliminate habitual nail biting.

"I now stop biting my fingernails.

"I release the desire to bite my fingernails now. I will be in control of my actions and avoid biting my fingernails. I allow myself to relax more…day by day…moment by moment…and *stop biting* my fingernails. As I *gain more control* over my body and my actions, I easily stop myself from biting my nails…and choose to just *feel calm* and relaxed.

"As I now discontinue biting my fingernails, my fingernails grow strong and healthy. I *feel better now* about my ability to control all of my actions when I decide to avoid fingernail biting.

"I picture stopping myself from biting my nails as I become more aware of my actions. As I notice my hands coming near my mouth, I remember that I am *in control* over what happens next…and instead of biting my fingernails, I see myself letting my hands drop to my sides— calm and relaxed. As I do so I feel a sense of freedom and control…and that feels better than biting my nails.

"From now on, I become very aware when my hands go near my mouth. When I notice that action, it will feel as though time stops for a moment…and in that moment I can *easily decide* to avoid biting my nails. Whenever I feel tension, I draw two deep breaths and release them slowly. This relaxes me…and I find that my desire to bite my fingernails disappears. Instead, I will *feel relaxed* and in control.

"Any habit can be changed. Any behavior can be stopped. Habits are simply programs running in the mind. Through the power of my subconscious mind using hypnosis, I instruct my mind to interrupt the program of biting my nails. I replace that program with a new program of personal power and control. In situations where I used to run the program to bite my nails, I will now take a deep breath and release it...and that will start the new program to feel a sense of calm and control...no matter what the situation before me indicates. I take a deep breath...and I'll feel a surge of confidence and power course through my mind and body."

(The Wake-Up)

"I will awaken from hypnosis by counting to five. When I reach the number five, I will become fully alert and wide awake. One...beginning to awaken from hypnosis. Two...becoming aware of my surroundings...feeling satisfied, safe, and comfortable. Three...looking forward to positive results from this hypnosis session. Four...feeling absolutely wonderful. FIVE...FIVE...FIVE...now wide awake and fully alert."

Supercharged Goal Motivation

The following suggestions are designed to increase motivation for a specific goal and to eliminate the fear of failure.

Special Instructions: Choose one goal to work on per session. The blank spaces in the script require you to indicate the name of the chosen goal.

"I now become totally motivated in my goal to _____.

"I will feel more successful when I accomplish my goal to _____. I will be happier when my motivation improves now to _____. I want to improve my life and my goal will help me to do that. As motivation fills me, I *enthusiastically work* on my goal to _____…and I look forward to receiving *all of the benefits* that will come with it.

"This goal is important to me, and I will take the actions needed to accomplish it. I am *100 percent committed* to my goal to _____. I let go of the fear of failure because there is no such thing as failure. There are *only results*. I can accomplish what I put my mind to, just like I am doing right now. By hypnotizing myself with my eyes open to increase my motivation to _____, I have already proven that *I have the motivation* that it is rising within me to _____. All of my thoughts and feelings are becoming *100 percent* geared for the goal to _____. I have *100 percent determination*. It has been incubating and now I give myself permission to want this goal to _____. When obstacles try to prevent me from my goal, I remember that I have a *100 percent commitment* to _____. I love the feeling of *100 percent motivation*. My desire to reach my goal to _____ is growing stronger and stronger…stronger and stronger…strong desire increasing in me now. That's a great feeling that I want to continue to feel.

"I imagine what it feels like to be *100 percent motivated* and work toward my goal to _____. I picture myself going step by step, doing what I need to do now…until I finish. As I take each step toward my goal, I become more and more enthusiastic. I picture myself finishing my goal and *feeling so satisfied* and happy with myself for remaining *100 percent motivated* for my goal to _____. I think back and realize that it was worth the time and effort. My self-confidence improves greatly…because I realize I can accomplish my goals.

"Every day, my motivation is increasing for my goal to _____. I let go of feelings of hesitation and fear, knowing that there is really no such thing as failure. There are only results. So I feel happy and excited about my goal. My confidence to undertake any task is increasing now. I can do it!"

(The Wake-Up)

"I will awaken from hypnosis by counting to five. When I reach the number five, I will become fully alert and wide awake. One…beginning to awaken from hypnosis. Two…becoming aware of my surroundings…feeling satisfied, safe, and comfortable. Three…looking forward to positive results from this hypnosis session. Four…feeling absolutely wonderful. FIVE…FIVE…FIVE…now wide awake and fully alert."

You're Getting Sleepy

The following suggestions are designed to help
you fall asleep easily and have a good night's rest.

"I fall asleep easily and sleep soundly.

"Going to sleep is a natural process. I am able to *fall asleep* easily whenever I am tired. I do not have to *try* to fall asleep. It is when I stop trying and *simply relax* that sleep will overtake me pleasantly and easily. I let go of anxiety and tension and let my body rest when I feel tired…and go to sleep. Deep…sound…sleep.

"When I get into bed and prepare to sleep, I will feel a sense of peace and restfulness that helps me to relax deeper and deeper. To help my body relax, I will use my imagination to relax each body part, just like I did at the beginning of this hypnosis session. As I close my eyes, I will imagine that I am on a large beach blanket and that I can feel the sun's warming rays caressing and relaxing each part of my body. I will start with my feet and imagine I can feel the warmth on my feet as I relax my feet. Then I will pretend to feel the golden glow on my legs. Then I will feel it on my hips and pelvis…then on my stomach. I will continue to imagine each body part bathed in sunlight until I finish with the top of my head.

"By the time I have relaxed my whole body, my breathing will be relaxed…so relaxed that I can feel myself relaxing just a little deeper with each breath. So I will measure how much more relaxed I am feeling by counting my breaths backwards from one hundred. Each number represents a deeper level of relaxation than the one that came before it. Thus, number by number, breath by breath, I will become deeper and deeper relaxed…so relaxed that I may even *lose track* of the numbers as I fall into a deep…sound…slumber.

"I will *automatically fall asleep* as I count my breaths backwards. When I do, I will *remain asleep* until my body is totally rested."

(The Wake-Up)

"I will awaken from hypnosis by counting to five. When I reach the number five, I will become fully alert and wide awake. One…beginning to awaken from hypnosis. Two…becoming aware of my surroundings…feeling satisfied, safe, and comfortable. Three…looking forward to positive results from this hypnosis session. Four…feeling absolutely wonderful. FIVE…FIVE…FIVE…now wide awake and fully alert."

Great Sex

The following suggestions are designed to increase the desire and enjoyment of sexual activity for either gender when desire and enjoyment have been diminished.

"I enjoy making love and feel relaxed and confident during sexual activity.

"Sexual desire is a natural human drive. It is a part of my human animal nature, just like the desire to eat when hungry. Sexual desire is like a hunger. It's nothing I need to try to feel or do. *Sex is natural.* Sexual desire is natural. I know that when I don't eat for several hours, I naturally grow more and more hungry…until the drive becomes *urgent desire.* My sexual drive is the same way. It naturally grows *stronger* and *stronger*…more and *more urgent.* My sex drive is a hunger, and my *hunger for sex* must be fed. Even now, if I pay attention to my body, I can *feel the desire* reminding me that it is there. And that sexual desire is healthy and good. So I allow myself to feel that way…normal… healthy…good…sexual.

"I will *feel pleasure* during sex on every level of my being. As I release myself from the chains of inhibition, my mind, my emotions, and my body will enjoy *sexual pleasure.* I let go of any subconscious desire to be impotent or frigid and I choose instead to *enjoy sexual activity*…because I deserve to feel pleasure. I also release any ideas that enjoying sexual activity is wrong, sinful, or dirty. I am an adult now, and I decide what is right or wrong for me. I replace those old, worn-out notions about sex with new and uplifting beliefs about sex. I believe sex among consenting adults is natural and good. Sex is fun. I want fun activities to last as long as I wish. I feel uninhibited as I engage in sexual activities…relaxed and confident. I permit myself to be immersed in feelings of pleasure, knowing that sex is natural and normal. I enjoy making love—and sharing in this way.

"I take my time during sex…letting it last so that *I can sustain* and enjoy my pleasure. Sex is not a performance—it is an activity of mind and body. My *body gets aroused* as my mind gets excited. I enjoy giving sexual pleasure as well as receiving sexual pleasure. I get pleasure when I give pleasure to my partner. I let myself receive sexual pleasure from my partner because giving *me* pleasure gives my partner pleasure. So I give pleasure and receive it during lovemaking.

"When I engage in sexual activity, I will have a sense of freedom because while I am enjoying the feelings and sensations of sexual pleasure, it's very difficult to think of anything else. While I *enjoy sexual pleasure* with my partner I will be totally present. I won't think about the past, and I won't think about the future. I will totally immerse myself in the joy of sex.

"Sex and making love is like an unfolding action/adventure movie. It starts with an exciting premise…and builds and builds in excitement. I engage in foreplay to build and build excitement. I take my time so that I can enjoy the unfolding adventure. As the story builds, the feelings get stronger and stronger…and I find myself *feeling more* and more passionate. I let the adventure build slowly to a climax…and the climax is full and satisfying.

"From now on, I relax during sexual activity. I let things *come easily*. And as the clothes I wear come off, this will act as a posthypnotic suggestion so that my inhibitions come off at the same time. I will feel the sense of *raw sexuality* filling my mind and arousing my body. I will get more and more pleasure during sex. Sex is fun. Sex is natural. I want sex. I enjoy my sexual feelings."

(The Wake-Up)

"I will awaken from hypnosis by counting to five. When I reach the number five, I will become fully alert and wide awake. One…beginning to awaken from hypnosis. Two…becoming aware of my surroundings…feeling satisfied, safe, and comfortable. Three…looking forward to positive results from this hypnosis session. Four…feeling absolutely wonderful. FIVE…FIVE…FIVE…now wide awake and fully alert."

Lose Weight

The following suggestions are designed to make the body leaner.
The loss of fat rather than merely weight is the objective,
resulting in pleasing and beneficial changes in body composition.

"I lose body fat safely and easily.

"I *begin now* to program my body and mind to change my body composition safely…so that I weigh less and become leaner day by day. The body fat decreases safely, melting like snow on a warm sunny day. The muscles of my body increase now, day by day, so that I appear lean and attractive. Lean and attractive. As I *become leaner now*, my energy increases, and I feel stronger and more vital. I will *move faster* and more comfortably. I'll become healthier as my body becomes leaner and leaner. I'll *feel more confident* as I am leaner and leaner. I deserve to look good and feel good.

"I see myself fitting into my clothes better—even fitting into a smaller size, because I am leaner and the shape of my body is more pleasing now. I can see myself being *more active* in all that I do because I am stronger when *I lose fat and become leaner*. I even *feel lighter* as the fat is melting off of me…letting go of excess baggage I've been carrying. I see myself walking proudly, confident in my leaner body, as I go about my day.

"I imagine myself standing clothed in front of a mirror now, looking at my *leaner image*. As I look at my face, I see that my facial features appear *more attractive now* that I am leaner. I imagine that I am wearing new clothes that I purchased to accommodate my leaner body. They fit my new, lean body perfectly. My body looks great. I look good in clothes now. I am delighted by the shape of my body in the new clothes. And as I now imagine removing my clothes as I look in the mirror, I notice how my body looks fit and lean. My waist appears smaller. The curves of my body are in just the right place, and I admit that I look sexier now that my body composition has changed. I can see more tone in my muscles. I look good. I look lean. Seeing how *lean and attractive* I look makes me feel good. It makes me feel free…free to move with grace and ease…free to do the things I want to do.

"I feel safe becoming leaner…I don't need to insulate myself with layers of fat. I don't need food to feel comfort. Feelings of safety and comfort come from inside me. Right now I feel completely safe and comfortable even though I am not eating food. I am at peace and I feel great love for myself. Food can never take the place of the unconditional love and support that I give myself. And as I feel this inner sense of self-respect, self-support, and self-love…I realize that I can feel this way at all times…I no longer need to isolate or insulate myself from the rest of the world. I no longer use food to protect me. I feel safe and comfortable, protected and secure all by myself. And this secure feeling gives me the power to eat the right foods in just the right proportions.

"Food is fuel for my body. It is nourishment. I no longer use food to entertain or reward myself. I no longer eat when I am bored. I do not use food to compensate for anything that is missing in my life. If I am unhappy about something in my life, I address the issue that is making me feel that way. I no longer use food to satisfy any other need or want.

"Food is fuel for the engine that is my body. I want to put in the right kind of fuel so that my body runs perfectly. So I stop myself from eating any food that might slow down my body. Instead I fuel my body with nutritious food...fuel that my body can burn cleanly and efficiently... fuel that will supply me with energy and optimum performance.

"Day by day I am losing weight and becoming leaner. I *gain more control* over my body and my intake of food. I relieve stress and tension without the use of food. As my body changes and I become leaner, I feel safe with my new appearance. I am completely safe and comfortable with my changing body. I *feel healthy* and eat and think only in healthy ways. As I become healthier and leaner, I feel a sense of freedom, and that freedom feels very good to me."

(The Wake-Up)

"I will awaken from hypnosis by counting to five. When I reach the number five, I will become fully alert and wide awake. One...beginning to awaken from hypnosis. Two...becoming aware of my surroundings...feeling satisfied, safe, and comfortable. Three...looking forward to positive results from this hypnosis session. Four...feeling absolutely wonderful. FIVE...FIVE...FIVE...now wide awake and fully alert."

Eat Healthy, Eat Right

This is an excellent script to use all by itself or
as an adjunct to the "Lose Weight" script.

"I want to eat healthy foods in just the right amounts for good nutrition.

"Healthy foods are good foods. I enjoy eating clean and healthy foods because as I now begin to select only nutritious, healthy foods to eat, I realize my body will become strong, healthy, and full of energy. And that's what I really want…to be strong, healthy, and full of energy. Even my brain functions better on healthy and nutritious food so that I can think with greater clarity. I will be more exuberant and feel more joy as *I eat the right foods.*

"I don't need will power to eat the right foods. It has nothing to do with will power, because healthy, nutritious foods taste very good to me. I will notice the wonderful tastes and textures of the *healthy foods I eat* and realize that they really do taste good. And there is such a variety of healthy foods to choose from…that I enjoy experiencing the taste of many types of delicious, nutritious foods. They are packed with flavor, vitamins, and minerals…and it feels good to eat these foods. I feel good about myself as I eat healthy…as I eat right. I feel a sense of self-love and self-respect when I decide to eat right. And by eating right, I mean that it is right for me…healthy foods are in my own best interest. They make me feel better and look better. And that's why I eat healthily…because of the way it makes me feel.

"I imagine now that I am sitting down at a table piled high with all sorts of foods. There are many fatty, sugary foods on the table, but there are also some very nutritious foods on the table. I imagine taking a bite out of one of the fattening, sugary foods. It tastes okay…but I find that after just a bite or two, I've had more than my fill of it. I throw the rest in the garbage can because unhealthy food just tastes too heavy, too greasy, or too sweet. Now I look at the healthy selections of food on the table, and I reach for one of them. It's a food I like and am familiar with. As I eat it, it tastes so good, so healthy…the way food should taste. I feel good as I eat it. I feel happy and proud of myself as I swallow it. I then reach for another nutritious choice, but food that is different from the ones I am used to. As I eat it, it tastes fresh and good. It's fun and entertaining to eat different kinds of healthy food in moderate proportions.

"I eat my food slowly and thoroughly. As I bite any food, I make sure to chew it many times before swallowing because I know that this will help my body to digest the food better and easier. I will extract more of the nutrients from the foods I eat as I chew more slowly and more thoroughly. Any time I notice myself eating too fast, I will become aware of it…and slow myself down. This helps me to enjoy my food more and to get more mileage out of each bite.

"Because I am getting the nutrition I need, I find that I automatically eat just the right amount my body needs. I don't need any more than that. I don't want any more than that. I eat exactly the amount of food my body needs for good nutrition. After that, my appetite disappears until it is time to eat again.

"And my body thanks me for eating the right foods…in just the right amount. My immune system becomes stronger and stronger. I sleep better. I awaken feeling energetic and happy. That's the way eating healthy food allows me to feel, and that's the way I want to feel. So choosing healthy and nutritious food is easy for me."

(The Wake-Up)

"I will awaken from hypnosis by counting to five. When I reach the number five, I will become fully alert and wide awake. One...beginning to awaken from hypnosis. Two...becoming aware of my surroundings...feeling satisfied, safe, and comfortable. Three...looking forward to positive results from this hypnosis session. Four...feeling absolutely wonderful. FIVE...FIVE...FIVE...now wide awake and fully alert."

No More Procrastination

The following suggestions are designed to motivate
you to finish mundane and important tasks.

"I now stop procrastinating and get things done on time.

"I will *get tasks done* in a timely manner from now on. I am willing and able to *set goals* for myself and *stick to a schedule* to meet them. I give my attention to all important matters, whether personal or professional. I am responsible for tasks I need to perform. I *stop delaying* what needs to be done. I can handle any task. I can choose to perform any activity without delay.

"When I see something needs to be done, I act immediately. I feel relaxed about undertaking small and large tasks, knowing that I can handle them efficiently and effectively. I will *get more done* in my life. Things I know I need to do, I do…taking each task step by step. I break large tasks down into smaller ones and perform each step one at a time. So instead of feeling overwhelmed, I feel relaxed and confident to start any project. Some tasks may be less pleasant than others…but I know that the sooner I start any task, the sooner I will be finished with it. I want to *start now* so that I can finish. I want to finish…so that I can forget about it and move on to a task I enjoy.

"I picture myself in my kitchen. There are many dirty dishes that need to be cleaned by hand. Although I'd rather go read a book or watch television, I decide to begin cleaning the dishes, one by one. At first the task looks overwhelming…because there are so many dirty dishes. But I find great satisfaction as I clean each dish one by one, reducing the dishes remaining to be cleaned. As I wash each dish I get *more and more satisfaction*…because I know that soon I will have completed the whole task. It's a task that needs to be done and it is for my own welfare. And now I see myself cleaning the last dish. As I do, I realize how good it feels to get the whole task out of the way. The task was not as large as I had imagined, and I handled it efficiently and effectively…and now I can go read my favorite book, watch TV, or do something else I enjoy to reward myself.

"I *stop procrastinating now.* I can handle each and every situation life hands me. Day by day I *feel more capable* of handling all of my responsibilities. I make the choice to *handle each task* in an efficient, timely manner. There is time for everything that I need to do as well as for the things I want to do."

(The Wake-Up)

"I will awaken from hypnosis by counting to five. When I reach the number five, I will become fully alert and wide awake. One…beginning to awaken from hypnosis. Two…becoming aware of my surroundings…feeling satisfied, safe, and comfortable. Three…looking forward to positive results from this hypnosis session. Four…feeling absolutely wonderful. FIVE…FIVE…FIVE…now wide awake and fully alert."

Stop Smoking

The following suggestions are designed to gain control over smoking in order to reduce and eliminate cigarette consumption.

"I discontinue the desire and need to smoke cigarettes.

"I am not a smoker. There is no such thing as a smoker. Smoking is a behavior; it is something some people choose to do. Smoking is not an identity. I will *never* again refer to myself as a smoker. Whether I choose to smoke or *stop myself from smoking*…I have the power. I have the ability to remove the false label of 'smoker' from myself now. I imagine that there is a big label written across my forehead that says in dingy gray letters 'SMOKER.' I now see myself ripping that label off my forehead. To my surprise, it comes off very easily. And now I imagine ripping up the label into little pieces. It disintegrates into wisps of smoke and disappears. The label is now gone…I realize that *cigarettes have no power over me.* They never really did. I just believed they did. But now I know the truth. I have the power. I am in control, and I can use that control to *stop myself from smoking now.*

"I am able to relax and feel calm without needing or wanting to smoke. I feel a new sense of freedom as a nonsmoker, and freedom makes me feel relaxed. I choose to have clean, fresh breath because I have *let go of cigarettes now.* My teeth become whiter…as my desire to smoke fades away now. I *feel healthier and cleaner now*…as I release myself from the imaginary need to smoke. I will have more money to spend on fun things now that I *stop buying cigarettes.*

"Each day as a nonsmoker I am breathing better. My health automatically improves, giving me a new zest for living, an amazing sense of freedom and empowerment. I am in greater and greater control of my life…as I notice how easy it is to *simply choose* not to smoke. I only thought it would be difficult. But I know how easy it is to *be a nonsmoker now*. It feels good to give my body the respect it deserves. My taste buds return to normal and my food tastes better as *a nonsmoker now*. I feel more social knowing that as a nonsmoker I have more social freedom and respect.

"I walk away from cigarettes. I imagine a table in front of me with a line drawn down the middle. To the right I see a picture of myself smiling and looking so relaxed…so healthy and so attractive. It's a picture of me without a cigarette. To the left of the line is a package of cigarettes that looks dirty and grimy, and I can begin to *walk away from cigarettes easily* now. I pick up the picture of the healthy, happy image of myself. I hold it to my chest…and I turn and start walking away from the table…walking away from cigarettes. I turn to look back, and the table with the cigarettes has gotten smaller and smaller. And I feel so good holding the image of the healthy, happy me…the me who is a nonsmoker. I realize that I didn't really give up anything…instead, I've gained my health, my freedom, my sense of self-respect. And it was so easy to make that choice. I will have absolutely no withdrawal symptoms because hypnosis allows me to bypass them. I am free. I leave cigarettes behind me.

"I imagine myself going to a good restaurant. A hostess asks, 'Smoking or nonsmoking?' I hear myself with a bit of pride say, 'Nonsmoking,' and the hostess takes me to the luxurious part of the restaurant…where the air is clean and the smell of delicious food is in the air. It feels great to be treated well as a nonsmoker. When the food comes, I notice how I can taste the flavors of my favorite dish so much better as a nonsmoker. I hadn't realized until *I stopped smoking* just how much enjoyment of food and of life I was missing until now. As I sit there with family and friends at the table, I realize that I am relating to them feeling absolutely comfortable and relaxed without a cigarette in my hand. I no longer need a cigarette to feel secure. I feel good about myself and my personality…and I *feel much more attractive* without smoking a cigarette. As I finish my meal, I feel completely satisfied without the desire to smoke.

"I am comfortable and relaxed without holding a cigarette in my hand. I am in control of my life, my body, and my behavior. As a result of not smoking, my confidence increases…and this enables me to be in control of my eating behavior so that I do not overeat. Instead, I just eat normally, enjoying the taste of my food in moderate portions. As a nonsmoker, I have more freedom and control over my life than ever before.

"It feels so good to take control over my own life and behavior. I feel relaxed and confident all by myself. I can feel attractive and sociable without a cigarette. I replace the desire to smoke with a desire to take deep, lung-filling breaths of air. As I breathe deeply, I automatically feel relaxed and recharged. And that's all I really was after in the first place…to feel relaxed and recharged. Now I know I can feel that way without a cigarette.

"When I see others smoking around me, it doesn't bother me at all. In fact, it only makes me feel stronger and prouder of myself. They can even get smoke in my face, and it only makes me feel sorry for them. They've got a problem they haven't quite kicked as I have. They can even offer me a smoke. And every time I say 'no' to that cigarette, I feel a sense of satisfaction and power well up in me.

"I am now a nonsmoker. The old label is gone. Cigarettes have no power over me; they never really did. I only thought they did. But now I know the truth: it feels good to be free; it feels great to be healthy. My choice is an easy one. I choose to be a nonsmoker and remain one to enjoy the benefits of more happiness and freedom."

(The Wake-Up)

"I will awaken from hypnosis by counting to five. When I reach the number five, I will become fully alert and wide awake. One...beginning to awaken from hypnosis. Two...becoming aware of my surroundings...feeling satisfied, safe, and comfortable. Three...looking forward to positive results from this hypnosis session. Four...feeling absolutely wonderful. FIVE...FIVE...FIVE...now wide awake and fully alert."

Stop Smoking Follow-Up

This script should be used after three to five applications of the "Stop Smoking" script. Use it for three to five applications or until you've stopped smoking.

"I am and will always now be a nonsmoker.

"I am now completely free from smoking tobacco in any form. Smoking is a part of my past and a part that I am glad to be rid of. It was a hindrance to my health, my life, and my happiness. That hindrance has now been removed once and for all because I am a nonsmoker now.

"Cigarettes were not my friends, nor cigars, nor pipe tobacco, nor any other type of tobacco. I may have thought they were my friends in the past until I realized they were poisoning me slowly but surely. Any friend who would poison me is really no friend at all. Someone who poisons someone else is a murderer, a killer. And I don't have friends who are killers. I don't want friends who try to poison me because they are not my friends. They never were. Smoking tobacco is my enemy. And I recognize my enemy and am no longer fooled by the appearance or packaging or advertising of the poison in tobacco.

"There is nothing glamorous or sexy about smoking cigarettes. People who smoke look very silly to me now. In fact, when I see someone with a little tube of tobacco and paper dangling from their hands and lips, it makes me want to laugh. It really looks stupid. Bad breath, stained teeth and fingertips are not sexy. And that's what happens when people smoke. And I feel sorry for those people because they don't know how ridiculous they look smoking a cigarette. And I realize they light up like robots…that they haven't recognized their enemy yet…that they allow themselves to be controlled by a dumb, silly weed that is poisoning them.

"I don't like anything controlling me. I am in control of myself. I don't want tobacco to control me. I don't want smoking to control me. And I now take total control over what I put in my mouth. I have no desire whatsoever for tobacco or nicotine in any shape or form. It is easy for me to say 'no' to smoking because I am completely free. I prefer to rely on my wit and charm to have a good time. I prefer to relax with a tall glass of pure water instead of a little tube of poison.

"I will drink lots of pure water in place of cigarettes. The water will help me detoxify my body. It will remind me of my commitment to a healthy body. And I now make fresh fruit my snack of choice if I decide to eat between meals. Eating fresh fruit is also a way to detoxify my body and to enjoy an activity during a break in the day.

"I see myself six months in the future on a vacation. I am walking on a beautiful beach with someone I love…someone who loves me. As I walk along the beach, there is a big smile on my face as I realize I haven't wanted or needed to smoke for the past six months. In fact, it's hard to believe that I ever smoked at all. It seems like someone else I knew who used to smoke. I am so happy now. I feel healthy. I can enjoy my relationship with this loved one so much clearer, so much better. I am more myself than ever before. I splash my toes in the beautiful ocean water. My eyes are bright and clear. I don't mind hugging and getting close because I smell clean and fresh and natural. I feel more free and alive than I have felt in a very long time. I am a healthy, happy nonsmoker. And I can't fathom ever smoking again.

"If I have any cigarettes, cigars, or pipe tobacco on my person, in my home, in my car, or at my workplace…I am going to get rid of them! Trash them. Throw them in the garbage where they belong. And when I do that, I will feel an incredible sense of inner strength and pride. Throwing them away will represent for me an irrevocable and final break between myself and the deadly habit of smoking. As I throw them away, I will say out loud in a clear emphatic voice, 'Good riddance!' That's going to feel very good. I will do this as soon as I can upon finishing this hypnosis session because I'm done with smoking. I'm tired of it. And now I have control."

(The Wake-Up)

"I will awaken from hypnosis by counting to five. When I reach the number five, I will become fully alert and wide awake. One…beginning to awaken from hypnosis. Two…becoming aware of my surroundings…feeling satisfied, safe, and comfortable. Three…looking forward to positive results from this hypnosis session. Four…feeling absolutely wonderful. FIVE…FIVE…FIVE…now wide awake and fully alert."

Total Self-Confidence

The following suggestions are designed to build
feelings of self-confidence in all general areas of life.

"I *feel totally self-confident* in everything I say and do.

"I am comfortable with new tasks…as I decide to *feel self-confident now*. I remain calm and relaxed in every situation as I learn to choose self-confidence now. I feel less and less tense and allow my true personality to shine forth…when I grow more and *more self-confident*. My body becomes stronger, more poised, and healthier as I gain *self-confidence now*. Every day and in every way my life will improve as my self-confidence increases now. I relax and trust my abilities and my intelligence…with *total ease* and *perfect confidence*. People no longer make me nervous or cause me to doubt myself because I armor myself with self-confidence.

"I am able to enjoy any activity with total concentration and effort as I *feel strongly self-confident*. As I develop this *easygoing attitude* about myself, my focus is on whatever I am doing or whatever I have to say…rather than on myself. I relax and think more clearly as I build self-confidence now. I undertake new activities without fear…letting go of anxiety as I feel totally self-confident. I release the fear of failure…as self-confidence becomes my new way of being. All negative thoughts wash away as they are replaced now with belief in myself. I no longer allow anyone to walk all over me because the self-confidence I feel enables me to stand up for myself. My self-respect increases greatly as self-confidence fills me.

"I picture myself after this hypnosis session getting up and feeling stronger, more powerful, and very confident. I see myself walk across the room…and I carry myself with newfound self-respect. I look in the mirror at myself. I look like a different person. My posture is good; my face shows an expression of pure confidence. I look like I am relaxed and confident…comfortable and self-assured.

"By the time I read the number five in the 'Wake-Up,' I will act as though I am playing a part in a movie. I am playing a totally self-confident character…someone who is relaxed and absolutely sure. I will pretend that I am very powerful whenever I speak or act. I will act as if I am absolutely confident. And as I pretend to be confident, moment by moment I will find that confidence has become a real part of my personality…I *always feel very confident now.*"

(The Wake-Up)

"I will awaken from hypnosis by counting to five. When I reach the number five, I will become fully alert and wide awake. One…beginning to awaken from hypnosis. Two…becoming aware of my surroundings…feeling satisfied, safe, and comfortable. Three…looking forward to positive results from this hypnosis session. Four…feeling absolutely wonderful. FIVE…FIVE…FIVE…now wide awake and fully alert."

Clear and Healthy Skin

The following suggestions are designed to reduce
or eliminate skin problems and improve the skin's overall
condition. Where a specific skin malady is mentioned, you
may substitute another word specific to your condition.

"I have clear and healthy skin.

"I want to look more attractive…as my skin begins to clear and become healthier now. As it does, my circulation improves…supplying my skin all the blood and nutrients it needs to be clear, healthy, and attractive. The texture of my *skin feels supple* and normal as any signs of blemishes and irritation fade away. My *skin is nourished perfectly* and contains just the right amount of moisture to keep it healthy and clear. My body processes waste material more efficiently from now on, and it stops manifesting blemishes on my skin.

"I will look in the mirror with confidence as my *skin is clear* and healthy. As I am *free of blemishes* and irritated skin, I naturally feel more attractive and become more social. I am less and less self-conscious about my skin…as it becomes and remains smooth and clear.

"I imagine standing in front of a three-way mirror, one that shows my body from many angles. My face and chest, as I look at my reflection, show clear, *vibrant skin*…with a healthy glow. As I look at the reflection of my back, I see the complexion there is clean and clear. Every part of my skin, from my head to my feet, is healthy and free of blemishes. My skin is beautiful, clear, and healthy.

"My skin is less irritable and *less sensitive now*…to environmental factors. My subconscious now finds healthy ways of eliminating bodily wastes and toxins other than producing blemishes. And as I learn to relax and *let go of stress* more and more with each passing day, my *skin becomes clearer* and clearer. I appreciate and approve of myself. I accept myself totally…and release the need and desire for problems with my skin. My skin is getting clearer and clearer…like the reflection of a calm, mountain lake.

"I am more relaxed about my appearance. I feel relaxed and calm about my life. I allow all tension in my mind to fade away now…so I feel calm and comfortable throughout the day. And because I feel calm and comfortable in my mind, my body feels calm and comfortable also. My body feels calm and comfortable, so I no longer want or need blemishes on my skin…because the stress is gone. It's gone from my mind and gone from my body. Everything is just fine. I feel good and healthy, so *my skin feels good and healthy.*"

(The Wake-Up)

"I will awaken from hypnosis by counting to five. When I reach the number five, I will become fully alert and wide awake. One…beginning to awaken from hypnosis. Two…becoming aware of my surroundings…feeling satisfied, safe, and comfortable. Three…looking forward to positive results from this hypnosis session. Four…feeling absolutely wonderful. FIVE…FIVE…FIVE…now wide awake and fully alert."

Hypnosis Script

Acing Exams

The following suggestions are designed to help reduce
nervousness and increase memory recall and focus during
an examination. Note that this is not a substitute for studying.

"I am relaxed and focused during tests and exams.

"I want to achieve the highest marks possible for me on my tests. I
want to discontinue any desires within me to perform less than I am
truly capable of...and I increase my desire and motivation to make
excellent marks.

"I allow my body to relax as I take any exam. My body is completely
safe before, during, and after any exam. I realize that in the past I may
have confused my body because of my worry, which led it to think that
there was some imminent danger to its well-being. It thought it was
doing me a favor by being on the alert and shutting off my higher thinking faculties. But now I'm letting my body know that there is no danger
to our survival during any written test. And although I want to do very
well on the test, my survival in no way depends on any examination. So
I now send my body a message of peace before and during a test.

"I will feel totally at ease as I take any test. Distractions around me
during an exam do not disturb my concentration. I ignore any distractions. My own train of thought remains focused on the questions
and answers to the questions on the exam in front of me. I *relax and
focus* with confidence...from the moment I pick up the exam to the
time when I turn it back in for grading. *My memory is excellent*, as well
as my problem-solving abilities. I have a *great ability to recall* information
and, as I relax during the test, information is easily retrieved

from…my excellent and *accessible memory*. My conscious mind and my subconscious are in close rapport at all times during the exam and work well together to answer any question on the test.

"I picture myself walking into the examination room, feeling relaxed and comfortable. Having studied for the test, I *feel confident and secure* that I will do very well on the exam. As I sit down and look at the exam questions, I suddenly feel relaxed and focused. My mind becomes clear, and I can *focus easily* on each question or problem on the exam. As I answer each question, the answers come to me easily and readily. I can even imagine finishing the exam with enough time to look over my answers. I thank my subconscious mind for allowing me to *stay relaxed and focused* throughout the entire exam…and for remembering all information needed to answer the exam questions correctly.

"When I sit down to take an exam and feel the chair pressing against my back, I automatically *become relaxed and focused*…with a high degree of concentration and memory recall. The feeling of the chair against my back puts in me in the *perfect mental state* for doing well on the exam."

(The Wake-Up)

"I will awaken from hypnosis by counting to five. When I reach the number five, I will become fully alert and wide awake. One…beginning to awaken from hypnosis. Two…becoming aware of my surroundings…feeling satisfied, safe, and comfortable. Three…looking forward to positive results from this hypnosis session. Four…feeling absolutely wonderful. FIVE…FIVE…FIVE…now wide awake and fully alert."

Sharp Memory

The following suggestions are designed
to help you have better recall.

"I possess the ability to recall all things with clarity.

"Starting right now, my memory is improving sharply. I let go of any desire to forget things. I find that I easily *remember names* of people I have met regardless of how long I've known them. I quickly *remember dates and places.* I effortlessly remember things that happened long ago. I *remember events* that took place a short time ago…in perfect detail. I trust my memory to *recall all things* when I need them.

"My mind functions perfectly. My memory is completely intact. My brain is like a video recorder and stores all that I've ever seen, heard, tasted, touched, or felt. It also stores all of the ideas I've ever had. The information is in my brain, and I have perfect access to all that it contains. It is my mind and my brain…and I choose to utilize its ability to retrieve information when I ask for it or need it. My short-term memory is perfect and clear. My long-term memory is there for me as I need it.

"From now on, whenever I need to remember any information, I simply relax, and the stored information rises to my conscious mind with vivid clarity. Day by day my ability to recall events and all information is stronger and quicker. I gain more and more confidence in my ability to remember anything and everything that I know. I am very intelligent and my mind is sharp and powerful. My memory and my ability to use it are excellent. I have *a sharp memory now.*

"My memory is like a video-recording unit. It remembers everything I see, and it remembers all that I hear…down to the last detail. I imagine that accessing a memory is like pressing the 'play' button on my home video machine. I can quickly and easily play anything I have recorded…anything I have seen or heard.

"My mind is like a very complex computer with unlimited memory storage. Everything that I've ever put into my mind is still there in the memory bank. All I have to do is think of a key word to access any memory or any piece of information. My mind is like a very fast and vast computer. I *retrieve information easily and readily.*"

(The Wake-Up)

"I will awaken from hypnosis by counting to five. When I reach the number five, I will become fully alert and wide awake. One…beginning to awaken from hypnosis. Two…becoming aware of my surroundings…feeling satisfied, safe, and comfortable. Three…looking forward to positive results from this hypnosis session. Four…feeling absolutely wonderful. FIVE…FIVE…FIVE…now wide awake and fully alert."

Intensify and Maximize Workouts

The following suggestions are designed to augment motivation and intensity during weight-bearing exercise and maximize results.

"I will increase my motivation to work out, intensify my efforts while I work out, and maximize the results of working out.

"I now achieve a powerful, lean body. Working my body with weights allows me to reach my desire, so my motivation to work out now increases. My motivation to *work out regularly* doubles every day. This increase in motivation to work out allows me to *work out more intensely* so that results come quickly. The results are excellent. My body is becoming fitter, stronger, and more muscular in all the right places. These are the results from my increasing motivation to *work out regularly* and with *greater intensity*.

"As my body gets fitter, stronger, and leaner, I *feel better* about the way I look in clothes and out of clothes. As I see the results of my *high motivation*, I feel pleased that I did something that was just for me…just to allow myself to feel really good…to know that I *have the motivation* and discipline to accomplish my goals. When I look in the mirror and *feel very happy* with my improved body, I feel satisfied that I've changed my appearance. I look sexier. I look more powerful. I am maximizing my physical potential.

"I imagine myself two months in the future…looking at myself in the mirror after an exhilarating, *intense workout*. I can see the change in my body, and the results please me very much. My muscles have filled out in all the right places…and I *feel very proud* of my body, my physique. I hear someone I know compliment me on how my body has changed in the last two months. It feels good to be noticed for my accomplishment. And I *feel so good* about my improvement…that I feel even *more motivated now* to continue working out with *high motivation* and intensity.

"When I'm resting, my subconscious mind restores and regenerates my body. I instruct my subconscious mind through the power of hypnosis to *maximize muscular gains*—to build more muscle and burn more fat…safely and efficiently. As I sleep, my unconscious mind will build my muscles…making them bigger and stronger than ever before.

"From now on as I lift weights during my workout, I feel a rush of motivation and intensity fill me. The weights seem lighter because my intensity is so strong.

"I *love the feelings* that take place during and after a good workout. I enjoy the *natural high* I feel as the endorphins rush through my body during and after working out. I *feel so alive* when I work out. I feel strong but at peace. I feel confident and sure of myself. My *body feels powerful* and vital. My mind feels relaxed and refreshed at the end of a workout. It's the most incredible feeling that keeps me coming back and wanting to work out regularly.

"I feel released when I work out. It's a time when I can let go of all other tasks and responsibilities and just do something for me…and that feels good. Working out feels good. And I like to return to that feeling regularly…so I work out regularly…to feel good. I don't *have* to work out…I *want* to work out. I like working out. I enjoy the physical activity…and I love what it does for my body and my mind."

(The Wake-Up)

"I will awaken from hypnosis by counting to five. When I reach the number five, I will become fully alert and wide awake. One...beginning to awaken from hypnosis. Two...becoming aware of my surroundings...feeling satisfied, safe, and comfortable. Three...looking forward to positive results from this hypnosis session. Four...feeling absolutely wonderful. FIVE...FIVE...FIVE...now wide awake and fully alert."

Strong Immune System

The following suggestions are designed
to support a healthy immune system.

"I increase the function of my immune system to fight off disease.

"I want to *be healthy* and happy and to enjoy a prosperous life. I empower myself in all areas of life, including my immune system. I now optimize my immune system to fight off invading organisms.

"I imagine my body is like a kingdom. I want to keep my kingdom healthy and harmonious. I am the ruler of my kingdom…and have charge over vast armies of warrior cells that fight and defend my kingdom from enemy invaders. I imagine that I dispatch special cells that are like soldiers armed with swords…seeking out invaders, unwanted viruses; my soldiers are smart. I call upon my army now, my T-soldiers. They are a special army…very strong and very powerful. There are *new T-soldiers forming* and training even now. I make more T-soldiers now…trained to attack invaders, uninvited barbarian viruses. My T-soldiers know the difference between healthy cells and invaders. And when they find invaders, my T-soldiers *dispose of the invaders*…quickly and expertly…so that peace returns to the kingdom…my kingdom…the kingdom of my body. And when my T-soldiers are finished ridding an invader, I send out special messengers that calm the T-soldiers after battle…and send them home…where they can rest up for the next battle.

"My health is important…because I am important. I am capable and I appreciate myself. I deserve to be healthy and prosperous. I feel good about who and what I am. The world is a better place because I exist. I am a good person and I deserve to be treated well…to be treated with respect. I deserve to treat myself well…to treat my body with respect. I give myself permission to have a *perfect and healthy immune system now*…a perfectly *healthy immune system now*. My immune system will function perfectly. My mind knows how to activate subconscious processes to *create perfect harmony* in my body. My subconscious activates subconscious processes to *create perfect health* and harmony now. Total health and harmony now."

(The Wake-Up)

"I will awaken from hypnosis by counting to five. When I reach the number five, I will become fully alert and wide awake. One…beginning to awaken from hypnosis. Two…becoming aware of my surroundings…feeling satisfied, safe, and comfortable. Three…looking forward to positive results from this hypnosis session. Four…feeling absolutely wonderful. FIVE…FIVE…FIVE…now wide awake and fully alert."

Rapid Healing

The following suggestions are designed to increase the body's ability and speed at healing itself because of illness or injury.

"I greatly increase the power and speed of my body to heal itself in every way.

"My mind controls my body. My subconscious mind regulates my body's ability to heal itself of injury and illness. My subconscious regulates the speed at which my body heals itself. In hypnosis, I have the ability to direct my subconscious mind to heal my body perfectly…efficiently…and to *heal more quickly*.

"I now commission my subconscious…to *heal my body* with greater efficiency. I direct my mind to safely increase its ability to *overcome illness* very rapidly from now on. I *overcome injury rapidly* from now on. I direct my mind…to direct my body…to *heal injury fast*…to restore and *regenerate healthy cells faster* now. Regenerate healthy cells faster now. I overcome illness and injury faster now…more efficiently from now on.

"My subconscious utilizes the resources of my body…like a biologist or a chemist. My subconscious is an expert in its own biology; my subconscious is an expert in the chemistry of my body. It knows exactly which chemicals…in just the right proportions…are needed to promote rapid healing—*rapid healing now*. I can imagine my subconscious is like a scientist in a laboratory…the laboratory of my body. I can see the scientist…a genius in biology and chemistry. The scientist has a big laboratory…with access to a huge pharmacy…the pharmacy of my body. My body contains every chemical and every cell it needs….It can create any substance or cell it needs…like an expert. I imagine my inner scientist hard at work…using scientific machinery and devices—it's carefully examining cells of my body under a microscope…deciding now which chemicals to mix and match in a test tube…to create a condition of *quick recovery* and rapid healing for my entire body. I watch as the scientist finds the antidote…the formula for quick healing…and pours the potent mixture into a long tube…a tube that leads to the part of my body that requires quick and efficient recovery. The formula will continue to be available for all current and future injuries or illnesses…so I will always heal rapidly—I am a *rapid healer*.

"My subconscious mind follows my directions now to create a condition…and send the message to every cell of my body…to *restore total health* quickly."

(The Wake-Up)

"I will awaken from hypnosis by counting to five. When I reach the number five, I will become fully alert and wide awake. One…beginning to awaken from hypnosis. Two…becoming aware of my surroundings…feeling satisfied, safe, and comfortable. Three…looking forward to positive results from this hypnosis session. Four…feeling absolutely wonderful. FIVE…FIVE…FIVE…now wide awake and fully alert."

Appreciate Your Mate

The following suggestions are designed to eliminate irritation about your mate and to enhance positive feelings about him or her.

Special Instructions: Wherever you see a blank, say your partner's name.

"I want to be more loving toward _____. I am now more loving toward _____.

"I decide now to let go of my own feelings of irritation about _____. I want to be happy in my relationship. I want harmony there. So I reestablish feelings of love and warmth for _____.

"I stop thinking about the little negative things—I let those thoughts vanish…evaporate like a small puddle of water on a hot sunny day. Instead I choose to concentrate on the wonderful qualities _____ has…the many wonderful times we've had together…the laughter and the good feelings we've shared. _____ does a lot of good things…and I now start realizing and recognizing every nice and beneficial thing _____ does…whether it's for me or for someone else. _____ really is marvelous—that's why I chose _____ in the first place.

"I think back now…when we first met…the first few dates we had…and I remember them as if it were today…the way I felt about _____. Just looking at _____ made me feel so incredible. Just being with _____ was a thrill. I saw what was and is truly amazing about _____. I had *no demands*…and I totally accepted _____ as an individual. I remember how much love I truly felt. I remember how much love I still feel now. I still feel that love now. I had forgotten until now…how much I really care about _____.

"I am not always perfect in the way I act toward my partner. I sometimes make mistakes. Some of the behaviors I do, some of the habits…some of the things I say…are less than ideal. But I accept that I am not always perfect…so I accept that _____ is not always perfect either. I am doing the best I can. _____ is doing the best _____ can. I allow myself to be human and I allow _____ to be human. It would be awful if _____ were perfect! That would place a lot of pressure on me to also be perfect. Instead, it's time to relieve the pressure and recognize now that it's okay that we both have our quirks…quirks that make us human…that make us lovable…that make us feel love for each other. Even imperfections can make me feel compassion and great love now for _____.

"I will be kind to _____. I will be gentler and more understanding toward _____. I refrain from harsh words. If I catch myself saying or doing something unkind…I will ask _____ to forgive me. I feel great love and warmth for _____, and I show that love through my relaxed and loving attitude now.

"From now on, whenever I find myself feeling tense, irritated, or annoyed in the presence of _____, I will become very aware of those feelings. I will then draw a deep breath and release it slowly. As I do, any negative feelings about _____ will be released as well. I will find that my mood is instantly better toward _____ I will remember how important _____ is to me and how many wonderful things _____ has said and done. I will realize that I don't need to be irritated with _____, and instead I allow the love I have for _____ to shine through me in thought, word, and deed.

"I love _____. I respect _____. I appreciate _____. I see the whole person. I am in touch with my tender feelings for _____. I want to express my warm feelings for _____."

(The Wake-Up)

"I will awaken from hypnosis by counting to five. When I reach the number five, I will become fully alert and wide awake. One…beginning to awaken from hypnosis. Two…becoming aware of my surroundings…feeling satisfied, safe, and comfortable. Three…looking forward to positive results from this hypnosis session. Four…feeling absolutely wonderful. FIVE…FIVE…FIVE…now wide awake and fully alert."

Creative Problem Solving

The following suggestions are designed to stir the
creative subconscious to solve a specific problem.

Special Instructions: Select only one problem to work on at a time.
Wherever there is a blank space, say the problem
or task to be solved for yourself.

"I think of a creative solution for _____.

"I am very creative. I believe in the power of my own mind to *find solutions* to problems. I begin now to *tap the resources* of my entire mind to find a solution relating to _____. Every problem has a solution…or more than one solution. My mind can form thoughts together in original ways and offer me a solution to _____.

"Any problem is actually an opportunity. This is an opportunity for me to *utilize more brainpower* to find a way to _____. It's a challenge and an opportunity…and I expectantly await *creative answers* to form in my inner mind and surface in my conscious mind. *The answers are coming now*…floating up…as if from a deep pond…coming up and breaking the surface of the waters…revealing to me the answers I need…the solution I want quickly and easily.

"I imagine that as I go to sleep tonight…my subconscious mind…will work on the problem and bring me a wonderful solution in the morning. The solution may show up in a dream, which I will remember. Or else the answer will simply come to me…seemingly out of the blue…sometime in the day. And I'll know that it was my subconscious mind…harnessing inner resources…that came up with the answers and revealed them to me. And that will make me so happy because it shows how well my conscious and subconscious communicate and work together…to supply whatever I want…whatever I need quickly and easily.

"I imagine now that I am the boss of a very efficient company in which every employee is a creative genius. These geniuses love to work overnight—they work while I sleep. My company of pure geniuses…has an overnight delivery system. I leave instructions asking my pure geniuses to *find a solution* for _____. I ask that when they find a solution, they are to send it to me…overnight express…so that I may have it tomorrow…the very next day…soon after I awaken. I wake up refreshed and relaxed…confident that my staff of geniuses…has come up with a brilliant solution and are ready now to *reveal it* to me. I have the solution now for _____."

(The Wake-Up)

"I will awaken from hypnosis by counting to five. When I reach the number five, I will become fully alert and wide awake. One…beginning to awaken from hypnosis. Two…becoming aware of my surroundings…feeling satisfied, safe, and comfortable. Three…looking forward to positive results from this hypnosis session. Four…feeling absolutely wonderful. FIVE…FIVE…FIVE…now wide awake and fully alert."

Hypnosis Script

Tap Your Creative Genius

The following suggestions are designed to bring out more
of your natural creativity and tap into your artistic side.

"I access my inner creativity.

"I am very creative. I am a very creative individual. I can and do express myself creatively. I no longer inhibit my creativity. Creativity comes naturally to me. I have a creative side to my mind and I give myself full permission to access the creative aspect of my mind.

"I disallow any inhibition of my creative self. I no longer let the limitations of other people inhibit my creativity. There is nothing childish about being creative. Creativity is as important as logic. I recognize that the true geniuses of the world combine their logical side with their creative side to express their genius. Creativity is as important to the world as logic. Creativity and logic work very well together. So I feel very good about setting free the creative genius inside me.

"I imagine walking down a long, dark corridor in my mind. At the end of the corridor is a large, locked cell door. Locked in the cell is my creative self. I want to free my creative self. So I take out a silver key and place it in the lock and turn it. I hear the tumblers move as the door unlocks. I open the heavy door and walk into the cell. The cell walls are all expertly painted with scenes from my life about which I feel strongly. I also hear music being played…a song that is the theme of my life. Sitting in the middle of the room is my creative double…who looks just like me but is dressed with creative flair. My creative double looks at me and smiles. As my creative self stands, we embrace…and I feel the creative side of myself merge with my logical side. We become one. I feel the power…the unity…of my creative and logical sides merging. We are together now. We are allies. I walk out of the cell and down the corridor at the end of which is an open door leading to the sunshine. And as I step out of the prison and into the light, I bring with me my creative self whom I allow to express creativity freely from now on.

"I now access more of my creativity. Creative ideas are flowing from my mind. I pay attention to them. I honor my creative ideas and express them perfectly. It doesn't matter what people think of my creative expressions. Some will like them. Some won't. Who cares? I express my creative side because it is in my nature to do so. It is a part of me that I have set free. I am a creative person."

(The Wake-Up)

"I will awaken from hypnosis by counting to five. When I reach the number five, I will become fully alert and wide awake. One…beginning to awaken from hypnosis. Two…becoming aware of my surroundings…feeling satisfied, safe, and comfortable. Three…looking forward to positive results from this hypnosis session. Four…feeling absolutely wonderful. FIVE…FIVE…FIVE…now wide awake and fully alert."

Make More Money

The following suggestions are designed to increase drive
and confidence to make more money, and to
eliminate negative beliefs about money.

"I have a strong drive and motivation to increase my monetary income.

"I release now limiting beliefs about money or my ability *to make more money*. I choose now to trust myself to make more money…to *earn more money*. I will use money for my own good and the good of others. Money is neither good nor bad; it's how people utilize money that makes it good or bad.

"I trust myself to use money in a good way. I can have more money and choose to be more generous. When I *have more money*, I can afford to be more generous…and do good with money. I treat myself better to things I want…things I deserve. Having material wants…material needs…wanting more money to meet those wants and needs…is natural and good. I can have what I want.

"I *deserve to have* anything I can imagine…and I can have it without depriving anyone else of what they want. In fact, the more money I have, the more money I can spend. When I spend money, I give the money to someone else…so they have more money to spend on what they want. So by having more money and getting what I want…I am helping others get what they want. And that's a good thing. I can help myself and help others when…I *make more money*. I want to make more money.

"I imagine myself in my castle, standing at a luxurious door made of silver…encrusted with jewels. I use my key to unlock the door. As

I open it, as I *open the door now*…I see a treasure chamber. The chamber is full of open treasure chests brimming with gold and silver coins…sparkling rubies, emeralds, sapphires, and other precious gems. There is a chandelier made of diamonds…and the bright sparkling light reflecting off the coins and jewels amazes me. The room is finely decorated with tapestries lining the walls depicting royalty. And as I look more closely, I realize that I am the one depicted in the tapestries. *I am royalty!* The treasure chamber is mine along with everything it contains. In the middle of the room is a large, golden goblet sitting on a table amid a cornucopia of fine food. I pick up the golden goblet…and see my own royal reflection in the polished gold. I now drink from the goblet of riches…and the ambrosia of wealth tastes good. I feel so good…I feel happy…that I've discovered my treasure chamber—that all of its contents are here to serve me.

"I live in an abundant universe. I allow myself to partake in that abundance. I recognize the abundance of wealth that is all around me in its myriad forms, and I allow myself to flow with that abundance. This abundance includes money and material supply. As I freely receive I can freely give to others that they, too, might share in the abundance of the earth and the universe. I accept more material supply with joy and thanksgiving.

"I am open to *make more money*. I am open to all good opportunities to make more money. I am careful and wise in my decisions to make more money. I draw the people and opportunities I need to have more money. I am smart enough to get what I want. I get what I want. I get what I want…as much as I want…in a moral and ethical manner.

"I now foster the thoughts and attitudes necessary to become more materially abundant and to *make more money now.* I allow my creativity to guide me to…generate a greater monetary income now."

(The Wake-Up)

"I will awaken from hypnosis by counting to five. When I reach the number five, I will become fully alert and wide awake. One…beginning to awaken from hypnosis. Two…becoming aware of my surroundings…feeling satisfied, safe, and comfortable. Three…looking forward to positive results from this hypnosis session. Four…feeling absolutely wonderful. FIVE…FIVE…FIVE…now wide awake and fully alert.

Part Three

6

Instant Self-Hypnosis
while You Write

Instant Self-Hypnosis involves two discoveries that are closely related to one another. In preceding sections, you learned how I discovered a method of becoming hypnotized while you read. This chapter is about another discovery I made that allows you to hypnotize yourself while you write!

How I Accidentally Hypnotized Myself while Writing

The discovery that it is possible to hypnotize yourself while writing actually came to me several days before I discovered hypnotizing yourself while reading. Yet I didn't realize the implications of either discovery until I experienced both.

To say that the discovery I'll now share with you took place early in my professional career as a hypnotherapist would be an understatement because it occurred on the evening before my very first paying client was due for her first appointment! Although I had successfully been hypnotizing friends and colleagues, I was a bit nervous about my abilities with someone who was actually going to hand me cash for the experience. Wanting to do a good job, I decided to write out longhand the entire hypnotherapy session from beginning to end. If that sounds like a peculiar thing to do, you're right. Most hypnotherapists at the very least repeat the progressive relaxation and induction portions of the session from memory. If they read from any kind of script, it is often only during the therapeutic-suggestion portion of the session. But I was not confident that I would remember everything I needed to say, and I figured that once my client's eyes were closed, she would never know that the entire session was being read to her from a script. Little did I know that my decision to write the entire hypnotic dialogue would lead me to an intriguing discovery.

As I sat on my comfortable couch in my apartment, I began writing the session's dialogue on one of those big yellow writing pads. I began with a wonderful progressive-relaxation exercise, one in which the client's eyes would be closed from the very outset. Then I moved on to a rather simple but effective hypnotic induction—one involving the visualization of going down a stairway. By this time, I found that I was very focused and deeply involved in what I was writing. I felt inspired as I began writing the hypnotic suggestions for her goal. Originally I thought writing the session might prove a difficult task. Instead, the pen seemed almost to be moving itself as thoughts easily came into my mind and then onto the paper.

At some point as I was writing, I thought I heard someone say my name. Absorbed as I was, I didn't give it too much thought or attention. Whoever or whatever it was could wait because I was enjoying the task in front of me. I kept on thinking and writing. Some time passed (I don't know how long), when I thought I heard my name called again. This slightly annoyed me as this time the sound of the voice was more emphatic. Nonetheless, I would not be moved from my concentration on my task. The client was due to arrive at 7:30 A.M. the next day and I had to finish writing this script. So I continued writing suggestions, absorbed in my own thoughts, my own world.

Suddenly a thunderbolt seemed to sound as my housemate exclaimed in an insistent voice, "Forbes!" I looked up from the writing pad to see him standing a few feet away from the couch with a furrowed brow. As I looked at him, I felt a strange sense of detachment from my environment as though my mind were somewhere else. I had a feeling of relaxation and heaviness throughout most of my body. He asked what I was doing that so absorbed me, and I found that I slurred my words as I struggled to answer him. I realized that I was hypnotized. I had unintentionally hypnotized myself while writing out the dialogue of a hypnosis session!

Any qualified hypnotherapist would recognize the aforementioned phenomena as common indicators of hypnosis, and I had achieved it without ever closing my eyes or uttering a single word. My discovery was truly amazing:

**Hypnosis may be induced and sustained by
writing a script designed for that purpose.**

The "Combination" Method

I didn't immediately realize how this method might be of value to anyone but hypnotherapists because it seemed as though one would have to know the ins and outs of writing a complete hypnosis script for the technique to be utilized appropriately. It wasn't until some days later, when I made the discovery that reading a hypnotic script also produces hypnosis, that I came up with the idea of combining the two techniques so that a person both reads and writes during the same Instant Self-Hypnosis session.

I devised a method that begins with reading (aloud, of course) a revised version of the induction, called the "Instant Self-Hypnosis Writer's Induction." After reading the revised induction, the reader is prompted to write self-improvement suggestions while remaining in hypnosis. When finished writing the suggestions, he or she reads aloud the standard "Wake-Up," which concludes the session.

The reading of the induction ensures success in entering the eyes-open hypnotic state while requiring no special knowledge of hypnosis. The writing portion of the hypnosis is restricted to the suggestion phase. During this time, the writer can compose suggestions for meeting virtually any objective—and the suggestions will be instantly absorbed by the subconscious mind!

The Power of the Written Word

The writing of your own suggestions while in a state of heightened suggestibility has a very strong effect on the mind. In a literate society, we often overlook the impact that writing down our thoughts, desires, and aspirations has on us. Writing is very powerful because it requires attention to our own words and ideas. It forces us to focus on what it is that we need to express. When we read, we are usually expressing someone else's ideas and thoughts even if they are congruent with our own. When we write, however, the source is always coming from inside us and our individual motivations. And because we see what we're writing as we write it, a boomerang-like effect takes place. It reflects thoughts back into our minds and further imbeds ideas or suggestions contained in the writing. It also forces us to organize our thoughts to a greater or lesser extent.

Writing in a normal state of mind is powerful all by itself. Writing while in a heightened state of suggestibility multiplies the impact of what you write...especially if what you write is in the form of suggestions. It's as though the moment you write the suggestions they jump off the page and send the messages back into your inner mind with amazing force. The power of writing while hypnotized, therefore, should not be underestimated. Done properly it can have a quicker and longer-lasting impact than other forms of hypnosis.

Extending Instant Self-Hypnosis to Virtually Any Goal

The combination Instant Self-Hypnosis method may be of particular value to you if the professional scripts in the previous section are not suited to one or more of your goals. The writing/reading method of hypnosis enables you to write suggestions for virtually any self-improvement goal. Even if a prepared script from the previous section matches your goal, you may wish to tailor it to your situation and motivations.

Creating Therapeutic Suggestions

You, like others, may feel that you do not have the confidence or knowledge to write your own therapeutic suggestions. To learn how to craft suggestions, study the structure of the suggestions found in the professionally written scripts in this book. They use several types of suggestions, and most of the scripts are written with a definite structure, which can be studied and imitated.

If you don't have the time or patience to learn how to craft hypnotic suggestions, a quick and easy alternative is included in the next chapter.

Instant Self-Hypnosis while You Write—Summary

- Hypnosis may be induced and sustained while writing a script or monologue designed for that purpose.
- The reading and writing techniques of Instant Self-Hypnosis may be combined to form an easy-to-use method for you to impart your own suggestions.

7

The Suggestion Template

Once I discovered the combination method of Instant Self-Hypnosis, I decided to devise a way to write customized hypnotic suggestions without going to a great deal of trouble. I created a simple fill-in-the-blank template that you can learn to use in minutes. I call it the "Customized Suggestion Template."

How the Template Works

The template is designed to be used during an actual Instant Self-Hypnosis session so that you write effective suggestions while you remain in hypnosis. The template acts as a guide to assist you in writing suggestions for any goal you've selected. It directs you to write suggestions by asking you to write positive statements in connection with your goal.

On the next page, you can see an example of how a "Customized Suggestion Template" looks when it has been filled in appropriately. The sample template is a slightly modified script I composed and used to help me successfully lose weight. Take a look at the suggestions I wrote, the kinds of words and statements I used. Note that they were written for *my* circumstances and motivations. When writing your own suggestions, you will be adjusting things to suit your personality and situation, but the general formula should remain the same. After you review the sample template, detailed instructions will be given about how to use it for maximum efficacy.

Customized Suggestion Template

State your goal succinctly.

I will lose ten pounds by May 12, 1998.

How will life improve when you reach your goal?

I will have a smaller, trimmer waist when I am ten pounds lighter.

I will have a leaner body when I lose ten pounds.

I will become faster in sports, like tennis, and I will be ten pounds leaner.

I will appear more attractive as I let go of ten pounds of body fat.

What can you see yourself doing when you reach your goal that you're not doing now?

I see myself fitting into slacks with a thirty-four–inch waist.

I see myself confidently taking off my shirt at the beach.

I see myself enjoying activities like swimming and running.

I see myself attending parties, with confidence.

I see myself moving quickly and gracefully on the tennis court.

I see myself buying more form-fitting clothes.

Describe a multisensory scene in which you obtain the benefits of reaching your goal. (Use present tense.)

I imagine that it's the middle of June and I am at Virginia Beach visiting my friends. We are sitting on some beach towels, having just arrived on the beach. I feel the ocean spray on my face, but I realize that I am feeling hot as the summer sun beats down upon me. So I remove my shirt with total confidence. My friends comment on how I've shaped up and how good I look, and I tell them that I am ten pounds leaner. I am aware that strangers are looking at me, attracted by my lean, fit body. As I get up and walk toward the water to take a swim, I feel very relaxed and confident about my body as I reach the cool surf. I feel lighter and more attractive. I find that I swim easier and faster now that I'm ten pounds leaner, ten pounds lighter.

What behavioral suggestions can you give yourself to help you reach your goal?
I have a strong desire to exercise for at least thirty minutes a day. My desire for sugary foods is fading, diminishing day by day. Whenever I eat, I find that I am completely full after eating half of my meal. I will stop eating two hours before bedtime.

(The Wake-Up)

"I will awaken from hypnosis by counting to five. When I reach the number five, I will become fully alert and wide awake. One…beginning to awaken from hypnosis. Two…becoming aware of my surroundings…feeling satisfied, safe, and comfortable. Three…looking forward to positive results from this hypnosis session. Four…feeling absolutely wonderful. FIVE…FIVE…FIVE…now wide awake and fully alert."

How to Fill Out Your Template

The previous example gives you a formula to study and follow. Keep in mind that for your own goals, the statements you write will be different than those of the example—although they should follow the same general structure. The following explains the template sections and clarifies what kinds of suggestions to write under each heading.

State your goal succinctly. The statement should be a very direct suggestion, focusing your mind on your objective. Under this heading in the template, write a single sentence concerning what it is you desire to change or attain. Choose only one goal to work on during each Instant Self-Hypnosis session. Be as specific and concrete as you can. Try to avoid ambiguous goals and statements such as, "I want to be happy." If your goal is feeling-oriented, such as happiness or confidence, include in your goal statement what it is you wish to be happy or confident about. For instance, "I want to be happy and optimistic when at my job."

How will life improve when you reach your goal? In this section, affirm with your will what you want and why you want it. These hypnotic suggestions reprogram the inner mind and rally strength of determination. Make simple "I will—" statements describing the benefits of achieving your goal. Although you may include statements that forecast improved feelings in this section, include as many statements as possible that note definite and tangible improvements that will result from your success. Finish each sentence by repeating your goal.

What can you see yourself doing when you reach your goal that you're not doing now? These suggestions automatically create mental images of a concrete nature, which act as powerful indirect suggestions. For this subheading, begin every sentence with, "I see myself...." Finish each sentence with an action statement—an action you can imagine yourself performing once the goal is attained. Make as many of these statements as you can.

Describe a multisensory scene in which you obtain the benefits of reaching your goal. This is one of the most powerful forms of suggestion of all because it involves detailed, multisensory imagery. Write a paragraph describing a detailed scene in which you imagine you have already achieved your goal. Include as many of the senses as you can and as many details as you can about the scene: how it looks, where it is, when it takes place, sounds, smells, etc. Also describe the emotions you feel having achieved your goal. Make sure you write everything in the present tense.

What behavioral suggestions can you give yourself to help you reach your goal? Statements made in this section are what are referred to as posthypnotic suggestions. They will help you overcome obstacles to your success. Think of the things you know you should be doing that will help you reach your goal. Then write suggestions to indicate a strong desire to do them. Also, think of desires or behaviors you would like to avoid or decrease. Then write statements that suggest that these desires and behaviors are diminishing. Be specific and write as many statements as you can. Make your statements as positive and affirming as possible.

The Suggestion Template—Summary

- The "Customized Suggestion Template" makes it easy to write therapeutic suggestions while you're hypnotized.
- It can be used for virtually any self-improvement goal.
- A real-life example was offered to demonstrate how to fill out the template during a session. Details were given to explain each section of the template.

8

Customized Instant Self-Hypnosis Sessions

In this chapter you will learn to use the writing/reading combination of hypnosis in a specific sequence to customize your Instant Self-Hypnosis sessions for any self-improvement goal. You will learn how to incorporate the "Customized Suggestion Template" featured in chapter seven into your sessions in a way that makes the process easy and fun.

How to Use the Combination Method

To use the reading/writing method of Instant Self-Hypnosis, take these steps:

1. Choose only one goal to work on per session.
2. Find a quiet place where you won't be disturbed for twenty minutes or so.
3. Begin each session by reading the "Instant Self-Hypnosis Writer's Induction" aloud, which is included in this section. Read it in the same manner as you did for the "Master Induction."
4. At the end of the induction—while still in a state of hypnosis—turn to one of the "Customized Suggestion Template" pages. (You will be prompted to do this.)
5. Write your suggestions as directed by the "Customized Suggestion Template" page. By writing in this book, you have all of your scripts in one place, which will be handy if you should wish to repeat your sessions in the future. (See note below.)
6. When you finish writing your customized suggestions, complete your session by reciting the "Wake-Up." This is included at the end of every template page.

Note: there is one blank template for your use included immediately after the "Instant Self-Hypnosis Writer's Induction." In Appendix B there are several template pages to accommodate many more customized sessions.

Repeating Your Customized Sessions

Many of your customized sessions will need to be repeated daily for up to two weeks in order to achieve satisfactory results. When you repeat a customized Instant Self-Hypnosis session, you don't need to rewrite the suggestions for the same goal! Once you've written suggestions for a particular goal, your filled-in template becomes a script, ready for repeated use.

To repeat a customized session, take these steps:

1. Bookmark your "Customized Suggestion Template" that corresponds to the hypnotic suggestions you wish to repeat.
2. Begin your session by reading aloud the "Instant Self-Hypnosis Reader's Induction" found in Chapter Five.
3. Turn to your bookmarked customized script and read all of the suggestions aloud just as you wrote them. You don't need to read aloud the section headings of the template. For instance, you don't need to read aloud, "State your goal succinctly."
4. Finish the session, as always, by reading the "Wake Up" aloud.

You will find that repeating your customized sessions is quick and easy. These follow-up sessions take much less time than the sessions in which you wrote the suggestions.

Ready for Customized Instant Self-Hypnosis!

If you've studied the sample "Customized Suggestion Template," and if you understand the combo method of Instant Self-Hypnosis, then you are ready to begin your customized Instant Self-Hypnosis session.

Relax and take your time when it comes to writing suggestions, and don't be concerned about whether your suggestions are perfect. Your subconscious mind knows what it is you intend, even if you can't seem to precisely articulate it on paper. The intention and the feelings evoked are what really matter when using this method.

The Instant Self-Hypnosis Writer's Induction

(to be read aloud)

"Feeling a sense of privacy and comfort, I allow the sound of my own voice to soothe my mind and body while I speak slowly and softly. My body is slowing *down* as though everything is moving in slow motion. With every word I read and every sound I utter I feel *more relaxed* and at peace. Moment by moment, my mind is becoming as *clear* as the surface of a calm and quiet mountain lake.

"As my mind clears, I use my imagination to *relax more deeply* while I read. I imagine that I am sitting on a comfortable chair on a beautiful beach. With my peripheral vision I see the golden sand that surrounds me and the waves as they crash on the shore. I hear the gentle and rhythmic sound they make.

"I feel a moist sea breeze waft over my body. I notice the warm sun on my skin. I feel its golden touch on my scalp, allowing me to let go of any excess tension in my scalp. All of my thoughts seem to *quiet down now* as I concentrate my attention on the sun's warmth on my face…on my cheeks…on my ears…and around my jaw.

"The healing light seems to caress my neck and warm my throat, allowing the words to flow easily and effortlessly from my mouth. It feels as though hundreds of tiny fingers of light are massaging my shoulders and my upper back as I relax—waves of warmth and relaxation cascade down…down my arms and out through my fingers.

"As I take a slow breath and exhale, I become aware of this relaxing feeling filling my chest (take a breath and exhale slowly). A golden-yellow radiance floods my solar plexus as I take another slow breath and release it (take another breath)…and a feeling of deep peace and tranquility fills my entire stomach area.

"I mentally scan my hips, pelvis, and buttocks…and let any tension or anxiety there be gently washed away by a stream of light. I become aware of my legs now…they are almost aglow as sunlight floods down through them. My legs feel so relaxed. Even my feet and toes feel warm and comfortable…warm and comfortable now.

"As I bask in the glorious sun, I imagine closing my eyes as I prepare to hypnotize myself. I draw three slow, deep breaths (draw three deep breaths). For a few moments I can see the glow of orange light through my closed eyelids. But now that light fades into a comforting darkness as I draw my attention inward…inward…toward the center of my mind.

"I imagine that I am approaching a tall, modern, and familiar building. I walk through the revolving door and step into a beautiful lobby. Inside the building stands a powerful, armed security guard who keeps the building safe from unwanted intruders. The guard looks at me with a steely glare but then recognizes me as the owner of the entire building. The guard works for me. I give the guard a confident nod and make my way toward the elevator.

"I see the reflection of myself in the mirrorlike surface of the elevator doors. I look relaxed and sure of myself. I press the down arrow and the doors of the elevator open. I feel very safe as I step into a spacious and luxurious elevator car. I turn toward the panel of buttons that indicate the floor numbers. I press the number ten, which lights up as the elevator doors close. The elevator car begins to move down smoothly through the long, deep elevator shaft…with a very gentle humming sound. I watch the numbered lights above the door as they change. Each number lights up for a moment as the elevator moves past the indicated floor. As the numbers change…one by one…I feel myself descending to a wonderful place within myself…far beneath the surface.

"One…I watch the numbers as the elevator moves down…deeper down with every number.

"Two…*deeper* beneath the surface of this great structure…down below.

"Three…by the time I reach the tenth number, I will be hypnotized.

"Four…I will be hypnotized with my eyes open…open to beneficial suggestions.

"Five…I feel myself descending…smoothly…effortlessly.

"Six…still watching the numbers change above the door…one by one.

"Seven…going *deeper now*…feeling peaceful and relaxed.

"Eight…I am safe…I feel calm…going down…*down*…*deeper* down.

"Nine…I allow myself to enter into hypnosis with my eyes open.

"Ten…the elevator car comes to a smooth halt as I reach my destination.

"As the doors open, I enter into a comfortably furnished reading room. A burning log in the fireplace crackles and blazes brightly, as though welcoming me into the chamber. I approach a very comfortable looking chair and sit down. I pick up a book on a small table next to the chair. I read the cover of the book, which says *Instant Self-Hypnosis*. I open the book and begin to read. The words address me directly and seem to jump off of the pages and into my mind. And here is what they say:

"'You are now hypnotized with your eyes open. You will remain in hypnosis while you write excellent suggestions for self-improvement. Your mind begins to now focus on your goal for this session. The suggestions, as you form them easily in your mind, flow from your pen onto the paper as though the pen is an extension of your focused mind. You trust yourself to make excellent suggestions. As you write each suggestion, the suggestion takes firm root in your mind and immediately becomes active. You will find this form of Instant Self-Hypnosis extremely effective and easy to use.'"

(Please turn now to a blank "Customized Suggestion Template.")

Customized Suggestion Template

State your goal succinctly:

_____

_____

_____

_____

_____

_____

_____

How will life improve when you reach your goal?

_____

_____

_____

_____

_____

_____

_____

What can you see yourself doing when you reach your goal?

_____

_____

_____

_____

_____

_____

_____

Describe a multisensory scene in which you obtain the benefits of reaching your goal. (Use present tense.)

_____

_____

_____

_____

_____

_____

_____

_____

_____

What behavioral suggestions can you give yourself to help you reach your goal?

_____

_____

_____

_____

_____

(The Wake-Up)

"I will awaken from hypnosis by counting to five. When I reach the number five, I will become fully alert and wide awake. One…beginning to awaken from hypnosis. Two…becoming aware of my surroundings…feeling satisfied, safe, and comfortable. Three…looking forward to positive results from this hypnosis session. Four…feeling absolutely wonderful. FIVE…FIVE…FIVE…now wide awake and fully alert."

9

More about Instant Self-Hypnosis

Now that you understand what Instant Self-Hypnosis is and how its method works, there are a few things you may wish to know that have not yet been covered. This chapter fills you in on some important details and answers some commonly raised questions.

Ensuring Success

The primary ingredient with any hypnosis is the motivation of the participant. If you really want what you say you want, Instant Self-Hypnosis can help you get it faster and easier. This sounds very obvious because you might assume that everyone wants what they say they want. Sometimes though, we only want things because our spouses, our parents, or our doctors tell us that we should want them. To increase the speed and duration of your results with Instant Self-Hypnosis, the motivation must come from you…and you alone.

Two other ingredients that aid success with Instant Self-Hypnosis are belief and expectation. You must believe that Instant Self-Hypnosis can help you achieve your goals, and you must expect results from your sessions. If I've done my job in explaining what hypnosis is and why Instant Self-Hypnosis is a valid means for applying it to your goals, then you have good reason to believe it works! Your belief, in this case, is based on factual knowledge, and that belief should lead you to expect results. Hypnosis has been used by millions to help them change their lives, and Instant Self-Hypnosis now puts this power at your disposal. So why shouldn't you expect excellent results?

Possible Objections and Limitations

While Instant Self-Hypnosis is a valid and effective method of self-hypnosis, it is not without its limitations. Here are a few:

Not effective for regression and revivification. The eyes-open method is excellent for most self-improvement goals, but it is not an efficient technique for regression or revivification. Regression, which is a vivid remembrance of some event (or series of events) that happened in the past, is difficult to produce during an Instant Self-Hypnosis session. Likewise, revivification, which is (essentially) reliving an event from the past, is very difficult to produce with any type of self-hypnosis. This may be due to the limitation of depth possible with self-hypnosis, or it could be that with the eyes open it is difficult to observe images that rise in the mind. This is just as well because it would be unwise to attempt revivification without professional supervision, for reliving some experiences can be traumatic.

Privacy needed. As you've already learned, Instant Self-Hypnosis has several advantages over traditional self-hypnosis, but it does require privacy. Some people find it difficult to find a time and place for themselves where they may read out loud unimpeded or without possible embarrassment from being overheard. This is a valid objection and, for these people, silent, eyes-closed self-hypnosis may better suit them. But at home, this problem can easily be circumvented by letting others know what you're doing. Tell them that you need twenty minutes alone and that the self-improvement method requires that you speak aloud. You may be surprised by their curiosity about what you're doing, and they may even want to try Instant Self-Hypnosis for themselves.

Not deep enough. The issue of hypnotic depth is sometimes raised in regard to Instant Self-Hypnosis. Naysayers may make the objection that the method is limited in the depth of the hypnotic states it produces and that traditional self-hypnosis can take the subject deeper. The truth is that the depth of the hypnotic state, regardless of what induction method is used, is often difficult to measure. Many people (myself included) have reported phenomena during their Instant Self-Hypnosis sessions that indicate they have achieved of a "medium" state of hypnosis as measured by highly revered hypnotic-depth scales. It must also be remembered that hypnosis is partly a skill. So the more one utilizes the techniques of Instant Self-Hypnosis, the deeper into hypnosis they will tend to go. Remember, too, that the depth of hypnosis is less important than the motivation of the hypnotic subject.

Not for the treatment of pain. You may have noticed the absence of any scripts in this book targeting the alleviation of physical pain…and there is a good reason for this. Do not use Instant Self-Hypnosis or any other form of hypnosis for the treatment of pain without first checking with your doctor! Pain is the body's indicator that something is wrong. Hypnosis can (all too effectively) mask pain without treating the cause, which could lead to future complications. So be cautious. See your physician about any pain, chronic or acute, and ask if it is advisable to apply self-hypnosis (or any other form of self-help) in your case.

Questions and Answers

The following are the most commonly asked questions regarding Instant Self-Hypnosis, along with helpful answers:

1. **How many times should I perform Instant Self-Hypnosis per goal?** Repeat your Instant Self-Hypnosis session once a day (per goal) until you are satisfied with the results. Sometimes it only takes one session to see excellent results. Other times it takes multiple sessions to reach your goal.

2. **What if I don't see results after repeating a session several times?** If you have repeated your Instant Self-Hypnosis session at least seven times and still don't see any results, make sure the suggestions you are using truly apply to your goal. Also see if your goal can be broken down into smaller goals. If your goal is too big, the suggestions might overwhelm or confuse your subconscious mind. If it can be broken down into smaller goals, center your

next session on the first of the smaller goals. When you have success with the first goal, move on to the second, and so on.

3. **When is the best time to use Instant Self-Hypnosis?** The best time to use Instant Self-Hypnosis is in the morning, just after rising...before breakfast or coffee. The second-best time is right before you go to sleep at night. For maximum impact, avoid using Instant Self-Hypnosis after a heavy meal or after drinking a beverage that contains caffeine.

4. **Are hypnotic suggestions and affirmations the same thing?** These days, positive affirmations are a common form of self-help therapy for both mind and body. This is a great trend from which all can benefit. But affirmations and hypnotic suggestions sometimes differ. All affirmations are suggestions to the inner mind and, especially when accompanied by a relaxed and meditative state of mind, are very similar to hypnotic suggestions in form and function. Affirmations, however, frequently target a general condition—such as overall health, prosperity, and happiness. Hypnotic suggestions used in Instant Self-Hypnosis target very specific areas of change and aim to change a behavior or set of behaviors directly. Furthermore, affirmations are usually all phrased in the present tense, whereas hypnotic suggestions may sometimes use the future tense. They can be used to change a behavior at a specific time. Having made this distinction, Instant Self-Hypnosis can easily be adapted to apply affirmations in a very potent manner. The hypnotic state produced by Instant Self-Hypnosis can dramatically increase the mental absorption rate of the positive affirmations. See Bonus 1 for more information on how to use affirmations to maximum effect.

5. **Isn't it important to phrase all suggestions in the present tense?** No. It is not important that all hypnotic suggestions be phrased in the present tense. In fact, it has been my experience that to do so can backfire. It can even cause the mind to reject the suggestions altogether. The inner mind is to be treated suavely and

with great ingenuity. Placing all suggestions in the present can be too authoritarian for the subconscious mind. Plus, some suggestions simply cannot be put into the present tense to make any sense. Posthypnotic suggestions, for instance, target specific times in the future when the suggestion is to become active. It's best to follow the example given in the "Customized Suggestion Template." There you will find a variety of suggestions—some phrased in present tense, some targeting the future.

6. **Can I make an audio recording of a session and then repeat it?** Yes, you can make a tape recording of your session and listen to it as a means of self-hypnosis—but this method is not Instant Self-Hypnosis. Listening to a hypnosis tape is a common and prevalent means of hypnosis and self-hypnosis, and listening to one of your own voice may work very well for you. But, as you've learned, traditional methods have their pitfalls. You may, for instance, find yourself falling asleep while listening to your recording. This has happened to me on many occasions. I realize that listening to an audio tape takes much less "effort" than using the Instant Self-Hypnosis method—but the dividends that Instant Self-Hypnosis pays will be well worth your time and energy.

7. **What if I don't feel hypnotized during or after the session?** You may not recognize the feeling of the hypnotic state for a dozen sessions or more. The feeling is not important. Hypnosis is a very natural state—one which you've entered many times without noticing it. The way you will know that your efforts have been successful is by the results you achieve in regard to your goals. When you suddenly realize that you no longer desire cigarettes or that you are finally losing weight with ease, you will know that it is because of your success with Instant Self-Hypnosis. Results are the true convincers for any form of therapy, self-applied or otherwise.

8. **Can I write my own suggestions without using the "Customized Suggestion Template"?** Yes, you can write your own suggestions. The template is included to simplify things, not to limit you. If

you understand how to write effective suggestions for hypnosis, feel free to do so. Simply apply the Instant Self-Hypnosis methods where appropriate, but write (or read) your own suggestions in lieu of using the "Customized Suggestion Template."

9. **Is there anything that can be used to enhance the effectiveness of Instant Self-Hypnosis?** Yes. Earlier in the book it was suggested that playing soft music in the background during your sessions may enhance your experience. There are recordings available made to specifically encourage, enhance, or even induce a hypnotic state. I recommend their use. Also, available at your local electronics store are devices for the hard-of-hearing that amplify sounds and have equalization controls to allow you to bring out the deeper resonance of your voice. When used with earphones, such a device can greatly add to the quality of your Instant Self-Hypnosis sessions. These devices can definitely augment your sessions, for the sound and resonance of your voice plays an important role in placing you in the hypnotic state.

Naturally, you are the final judge of which self-help technologies work best. If you find Instant Self-Hypnosis works well for you, stick with it. If, however, you find the traditional methods and audio tapes preferable, that's okay too! The point of Instant Self-Hypnosis is not to negate or replace other methods of hypnosis and self-hypnosis. It's to give an effective alternative to their approach.

It's Up to You

You should now understand why Instant Self-Hypnosis is a breakthrough innovation in the self-help genre. Instant Self-Hypnosis gives you a powerful, quick, and easy-to-use method for changing your life, and you are the one who decides whether to put it into practice. No self-improvement method, no matter how simple and effective, will work unless you decide to use it. You have the final word.

Bonus 1

How to Supercharge
Your Affirmations

Early in this book, I mentioned affirmations as an inefficient means of self-change. But since so many people use affirmations, I thought I'd offer some further insights and an idea to make them much more effective.

Affirmations are suggestions to the mind. I think they were made most famous by a character on *Saturday Night Live*, Stuart Smalley, played by Al Franken. Remember him? He used to sit sappily in front of a mirror saying, "I'm good enough. I'm smart enough, and dog-gone it, people like me." It was funny...and silly. But affirmations needn't be either silly or funny. The problem with many affirmation users is that (as I've said) it takes too many repetitions to see any results at all. One reason for this is that the mind, unless in a state of heightened suggestibility, tends to reject the affirmations even when they are repeated. The other is that affirmations often don't contain a specifically stated outcome. It is not enough to tell yourself simply that you are "smart enough," for example. Your inner mind may reject the idea because you are being too vague, and your affirmation brings up too many other questions that are left unanswered. Smart about what? Book smart? Street smart? Smart dresser? Smart compared to whom? If your subconscious isn't given enough info to make good deductions, it probably won't respond to your affirmations at all.

That's not to say that affirmations are always a waste of time. But there is a way to make affirmations stronger and a way to make the mind much more likely to absorb them. To make them stronger, it is wise, if possible, to attach the affirmation to some specific visual imagery appropriate for it. You may already be using or working with affirmations. Good for you! There's no need to throw them out because they haven't been working as well as you had hoped. Instead, think about in which settings these affirmations are going to benefit you. Write them down. Be specific. So if your affirmation is, "I am smart," write a description of where and how you see yourself using your smarts. At work? In social conversations? This kind of specificity will enhance the emotional impact of your affirmation. Then to apply it to your mind with more punch, use any Instant Self-Hypnosis induction before you read the affirmation. Always follow up with the "Wake-Up." To make things even easier, just turn the "Customized Suggestion Template" into a "Customized Affirmation Template." Where the template asks you to state your goal, write down your affirmation. Then fill in the rest, as appropriate, paying extra attention to where it asks you for a multisensory description. For affirmations, you may disregard the template's request for behavioral changes, if you wish.

Bonus 2

How to Instantly Hypnotize Others

Now that you understand the basics of hypnosis and of Instant Self-Hypnosis, did you know that you have the knowledge and ability to hypnotize a friend or partner? You may have a mate or friend who is as interested in hypnosis and self-improvement. I will now reveal a simple method whereby you can hypnotize another person quickly and easily.

Instant Self-Hypnosis techniques make it very easy for you to practice hypnosis on another person, since these same scripts can easily be used to hypnotize another person while you read them aloud. All you need to do is to insert the pronoun *you* wherever you read an *I*. For example, where the induction script says, "I feel very relaxed and at peace," you would read to your hypnosis partner, "You feel very relaxed and at peace." At the end of the induction, you merely turn to the therapeutic script of your partner's choice and keep reading, continuing to say "you" instead of "I."

Do you see how easy that is?

You may even wish to take turns hypnotizing each other—becoming partners in hypnosis, you might say. Of course, before you begin, your partner should know the basics of hypnosis, just like you do. The most important thing for your hypnosis buddy to know is what to expect and what not to expect. You should have your partner read the section on the misconceptions of hypnosis. Once the basics are understood, you may take your partner through the "Master Induction" as an introduction. Just have your partner sit in a comfortable chair, close his or her eyes, and listen to you. (In this type of hypnosis, it will be easier for both of you to relax if your partner closes his or her eyes so that you don't feel watched and so that neither of you feel self-conscious.) Once your partner's eyes are closed, just read the "Master Induction" from Part One, but exchange the word *you* for *I* wherever appropriate. Read the narrative nice and slow with a lulling cadence, just like you did for yourself. After you've completed the part about the elevator, have gone through the complete count of one to ten, and have said your partner is now hypnotized, skip over the bit about eyes-open hypnosis (as this will not apply). Instead, go directly to the "Wake-Up" at the end.

After the induction, your partner will be ready to choose a specific goal from the scripts provided in part two. Once a script is selected, bookmark it, and you can begin hypnotizing your partner by reading the "Instant Self-Hypnosis Reader's Induction." Again, you will have to insert *you* wherever *I* is used. When you come to the end of the induction, you will omit the sentences about eyes-open hypnosis and about reading the scripts. Instead, you'll just flip to the page where your bookmark is located and begin reading the suggestions. Again, don't forget to read the "Wake-Up." After that, you've finished for the day. You should repeat the hypnosis once a day until you see results.

If you like, you can sit and close your eyes while your partner reads and hypnotizes you. It's a lot of fun.

Bonus 3

The Instant Self-Hypnosis Stress-Buster Challenge

Do you experience stress in your life? Duh! Who doesn't? I'm sure you know that stress can contribute to the lowering of your immune system and lead to all kinds of diseases of body and mind. In fact, I will tell you as a clinical hypnotherapist that just alleviating a client's tension level using hypnosis often dissolves their troubling condition or issue. Some problems vanish entirely when the high level of stress is removed. Stress, tension, and anxiety have a very real effect on you—probably more than you even realize, and yet it's up to you to do something about it. Yet in the frantic-paced world in which some of us live, it can be difficult to find time and cost-efficient ways to reduce stress. A trip to the spa can be costly. A massage takes too much time. Meditation (let's face it) is boring. But you now have a solution at your fingertips, and it won't cost you anymore money...and it will only take you fifteen minutes a day for the next seven days. I call it the "Stress-Buster Challenge."

Taking the challenge is very simple. First, you'll need to read Part One of this book and go through the hypnotic primer. This won't take you very long. Then, instead of using Instant Self-Hypnosis for some other goal you may have, use the "Stop Stressing Out" script found in Chapter Five. It's short. It's fast. Use it once a day for seven consecutive days, then notice how you feel! After seven days, I challenge you *not* to feel great—more relaxed with life and with yourself. Life will be more fun. Big problems won't seem so big anymore and little ones will seem laughable. You may even discover some problems seem to vanish because it was stress that created them in the first place!

When you finish the seven days, you can move on to using Instant Self-Hypnosis for your other goals. The challenge will actually help you to achieve those goals even faster. In fact, you may like the way you feel so much that you go way beyond the seven-day challenge. You may find yourself applying it every day! Believe me, it will do more for you than watching CNN or reading the daily newspaper. Don't worry, though. Everyone at work will be glad to fill you in on all the latest bad news from around the world. The great thing is that it won't bother you nearly so much as it used to because you're doing something to help yourself...body, mind, and soul. You're using Instant Self-Hypnosis...and your life's getting better and better every day.

Bonus 4

How to Deepen Your Hypnotic State

If you wish to experience a deeper level of self-hypnosis (and are willing to spend an extra five minutes during your hypnosis session), then use the following script. It is to be used after the Reader's (or Writer's) Induction, but before using a script or suggestion template. Simply bookmark the "Deepening Script" in addition to the script pertaining to your goal. Then begin reading the induction. When you come to the end of the induction, turn to the "Deepening Script" and read it aloud. At the end of it, turn to the script for your goal and continue reading. Remember to read slowly in a steady, calming tone of voice. Also, you do not need to read aloud what is written in parentheses, but follow the directions as indicated.

Deepening Script

(read aloud)

"I take my time and *now deepen* my level of self-hypnosis.

"I will imagine in my mind, even as I am reading out loud, that I am standing in front of a blackboard such as I would find in a school. I see myself holding in one hand a piece of chalk. In the other hand, I hold an eraser.

"I picture myself, to the best of my ability now, writing the letter *A* on the blackboard. I see my hand make the movements in my mind. I write the letter in my own handwriting (picture this without closing your eyes). I now picture myself erasing the letter *A* with the eraser in my other hand…so that just the blackboard remains (imagine this without closing your eyes).

"Now, I see myself beginning to write the letter *B* on the blackboard in my own handwriting. I take the time to picture this with my eyes open, knowing that I have a good imagination and that this is no different from the way I picture things when I read a good novel. Once I can see it in my mind, I now erase it with the eraser in my imagination (imagine it). And I realize that now that it is erased, I feel a little *more relaxed.*

"I will now continue to imagine writing the letters of the alphabet on a blackboard, one letter at a time, and erasing them. With each letter I write and erase, I allow myself to relax a little deeper. I will do this slowly and carefully so that each successive letter becomes more vivid in my mind's eye than the previous one. I will continue this until I finish writing and erasing the letter *H*.

"I continue now with the letter *C* (imagine writing it on the board and erasing it.)

"Now the letter *D*...I am relaxing deeper.

"The letter *E*...deeper at peace.

"Now *F*...I feel calm and tranquil.

"*G*...I am very relaxed.

"Finally, the letter *H,* as in *hypnosis.*

"I am now deeply hypnotized. I am open to positive change. I am now ready to impart helpful suggestions to my inner mind."

(Please turn to your selected script.)

Appendix A: Alternative Induction

"Feeling a sense of privacy and comfort, I allow the sound of my own voice to soothe my mind and body while I speak slowly and softly. My body is slowing *down* as though everything is in slow motion. With every word I read and every sound I utter, I feel *more relaxed* and at peace. Moment by moment my mind is becoming as *clear* as the surface of a calm and quiet mountain lake.

"As my mind clears, I use my imagination to *relax more deeply* while I read. I imagine that I am sitting on a comfortable chair on a beautiful beach. With my peripheral vision I see sand that surrounds me and the waves as they crash on the shore. I hear the gentle and rhythmic sound they make.

"I feel a moist sea breeze waft over my body. I notice the warm sun on my skin. I feel its golden touch on my scalp, allowing me to let go of any excess tension in my scalp. All of my thoughts seem to *quiet down now* as I concentrate my attention on the sun's warmth on my face…on my cheeks…on my ears…and around my jaw.

"The healing light seems to caress my neck and warm my throat, allowing the words to flow easily and effortlessly from my mouth. It feels as though hundreds of tiny fingers of light are massaging my shoulders and my upper back as I relax—waves of warmth and relaxation cascade down…down my arms and out through my fingers.

"As I take a slow breath and exhale, I become aware of this relaxing feeling filling my chest (take a breath and exhale slowly). A golden-yellow radiance floods my solar plexus as I take another slow breath and release it (take another breath)….And a feeling of *deep peace* and tranquility fills my entire stomach area.

"I mentally scan my hips, pelvis, and buttocks…and let any tension or anxiety there be gently washed away by a stream of light. I become aware of my legs now…they are almost aglow as sunlight floods down through them. My legs feel so relaxed. Even my feet and toes feel warm and comfortable…warm and comfortable now.

"As I bask in the glorious sun, I imagine closing my eyes as I prepare to hypnotize myself. I draw three slow deep breaths (draw three deep breaths). For a few moments I can see the glow of orange light through my closed eyelids. But now that light fades into a comforting darkness as I draw my attention inward…inward…toward the center of my mind.

"Now that my body feels *relaxed* and my mind is able to *focus* perfectly, I imagine myself standing next to a tall oak tree in the center of a meadow full of clover. The sun shines warmly on my skin. The sky is clear and blue. Beyond the meadow I see a forest. I look down at my bare feet and begin walking through the soft meadow, heading toward the forest. Startled rabbits bound and scamper through the meadow as I walk, and I soon find myself standing at the edge of the forest.

"There is a path leading into the forest, and at the foot of the path I discover a pair of comfortable-looking sandals. I slip the sandals on and discover that they are a perfect fit. They make my feet and legs feel very comfortable, so they are perfect for walking. The forest looks so enchanting and peaceful that I begin moving down the shady path. I notice the path is lined with willow trees. The deeper into the forest I now go, the more *relaxed* I feel. The air is perfumed with the fragrance of honeysuckle. Looking at fresh flowers in bloom always makes me *feel so good.* So I admire patches of beautiful violets as I walk by them. They are so beautiful, and *I feel so relaxed*, so good, so comfortable, just like I knew I would.

"As I come to a huge clearing at the very center of the forest, I see a magnificent, powerful castle up ahead at the top of a hill. As I walk toward the castle, step by step, I admire the beauty and majesty of the great structure, and I am filled with a sense of wonder and expectation.

"As I get closer and closer, I cross a drawbridge that leads over a moat and up to two huge, closed, wooden doors. Standing outside the doors is a formidable looking knight, fully armed and armored, who guards the doors. As the knight peers at me, a look of recognition and respect take over the knight's features. The knight then bows and says to me, 'Welcome back to your castle, Your Majesty.' As the guard opens the great doors and I walk inside, I realize that the castle is mine, that the guard serves and protects me, and that I have *complete access* to the interior of the fortress. For this is my castle…the castle of my inner mind. I am at home here. I am safe, and I am at peace here and now.

"As I walk through finely crafted and decorated corridors and pass by finely woven tapestries that depict scenes of beauty and harmony, I find myself at the top of a royally carpeted staircase leading down to the deeper levels of my castle—to the deeper levels of my mind. There are ten stairs, and with every step I count, *I go deeper* into the depths of my inner mind. And by the time I reach the tenth step, I will be in a state of hypnosis.

"*One*…I walk down the steps safely, easily…one step at a time.

"*Two*…seeing the stairs, the stairway in my mind, I feel myself descending.

"*Three*…each step taking me deeper down…deeper down now.

"*Four*…deeper down the deep stairwell of my…subconscious now.

"*Five*…down…beneath the surface…as I go deeper down—and farther in.

"*Six*…going deeper down, descending toward the deep inner chambers.

"*Seven*…step by step taking me down…down…deeper levels.

"*Eight*…the steps are mine, and I feel comfortable here.

"*Nine*…almost to the bottom of the stairs…to the foundations of my castle.

"*Ten*…I am now hypnotized.

"As I reach the tenth step, I enter into a comfortably furnished reading room. A burning log in the fireplace crackles and blazes brightly, as though welcoming me into the chamber. I approach a very comfortable-looking chair and sit down. I pick up a book on a small table next to the chair. I read the cover of the book, which says *Instant Self-Hypnosis.* I open the book and begin to read. The words address me directly and seem to lift from the pages and into my mind. And here is what they say:

"'Every time you read this hypnotic induction, you will go deeper into hypnosis than on the previous reading. You are now able to read and write excellent hypnotic suggestions. Your mind begins to now focus on your goal for this session. You easily remain in hypnosis as you read and write hypnotic suggestions. As you read or write each suggestion, the suggestion takes firm root in your mind and immediately becomes active.'"

(If this is your first reading, read the "Wake Up" below. Otherwise, continue by reading or writing the script of your choice)

(The Wake-Up)

"I will awaken from hypnosis by counting to five. When I reach the number five, I will become fully alert and wide awake. One...beginning to awaken from hypnosis. Two...becoming aware of my surroundings. Three...feeling the natural sensations of my body as it is awakening. Four...feeling absolutely wonderful. FIVE...FIVE...FIVE...now wide awake and fully alert."

Appendix B: Customized Suggestion Templates

State your goal succinctly:

_____

_____

_____

_____

_____

_____

_____

How will life improve when you reach your goal?

_____

_____

_____

_____

_____

_____

_____

What can you see yourself doing when you reach your goal?

_____

_____

_____

_____

_____

_____

_____

Describe a multisensory scene in which you obtain the benefits of reaching your goal. (Use present tense.)

_____

_____

_____

_____

_____

_____

_____

_____

_____

What behavioral suggestions can you give yourself to help you reach your goal?

_____

_____

_____

_____

_____

(The Wake-Up)

"I will awaken from hypnosis by counting to five. When I reach the number five, I will become fully alert and wide awake. One…beginning to awaken from hypnosis. Two…becoming aware of my surroundings…feeling satisfied, safe, and comfortable. Three…looking forward to positive results from this hypnosis session. Four…feeling absolutely wonderful. FIVE…FIVE…FIVE…now wide awake and fully alert."

Customized Suggestion Template

State your goal succinctly:

_____

_____

_____

_____

_____

_____

_____

How will life improve when you reach your goal?

_____

_____

_____

_____

_____

_____

_____

What can you see yourself doing when you reach your goal?

_____

_____

_____

_____

_____

_____

_____

Describe a multisensory scene in which you obtain the benefits of reaching your goal. (Use present tense.)

_____

_____

_____

_____

_____

_____

_____

_____

_____

What behavioral suggestions can you give yourself to help you reach your goal?

_____

_____

_____

_____

_____

(The Wake-Up)

"I will awaken from hypnosis by counting to five. When I reach the number five, I will become fully alert and wide awake. One…beginning to awaken from hypnosis. Two…becoming aware of my surroundings…feeling satisfied, safe, and comfortable. Three…looking forward to positive results from this hypnosis session. Four…feeling absolutely wonderful. FIVE…FIVE…FIVE…now wide awake and fully alert."

Customized Suggestion Template

State your goal succinctly:

_____

_____

_____

_____

_____

_____

_____

How will life improve when you reach your goal?

_____

_____

_____

_____

_____

_____

_____

What can you see yourself doing when you reach your goal?

_____

_____

_____

_____

_____

_____

_____

Describe a multisensory scene in which you obtain the benefits of reaching your goal. (Use present tense.)

_____

_____

_____

_____

_____

_____

_____

_____

_____

_____

What behavioral suggestions can you give yourself to help you reach your goal?

_____

_____

_____

_____

_____

(The Wake-Up)

"I will awaken from hypnosis by counting to five. When I reach the number five, I will become fully alert and wide awake. One…beginning to awaken from hypnosis. Two…becoming aware of my surroundings…feeling satisfied, safe, and comfortable. Three…looking forward to positive results from this hypnosis session. Four…feeling absolutely wonderful. FIVE…FIVE…FIVE…now wide awake and fully alert."

Customized Suggestion Template

State your goal succinctly:

_____

_____

_____

_____

_____

_____

How will life improve when you reach your goal?

_____

_____

_____

_____

_____

_____

What can you see yourself doing when you reach your goal?

_____

_____

_____

_____

_____

_____

Describe a multisensory scene in which you obtain the benefits of reaching your goal. (Use present tense.)

_____

_____

_____

_____

_____

_____

_____

_____

_____

_____

What behavioral suggestions can you give yourself to help you reach your goal?

_____

_____

_____

_____

_____

(The Wake-Up)

"I will awaken from hypnosis by counting to five. When I reach the number five, I will become fully alert and wide awake. One…beginning to awaken from hypnosis. Two…becoming aware of my surroundings…feeling satisfied, safe, and comfortable. Three…looking forward to positive results from this hypnosis session. Four…feeling absolutely wonderful. FIVE…FIVE…FIVE…now wide awake and fully alert."

Customized Suggestion Template

State your goal succinctly:

_____

_____

_____

_____

_____

_____

_____

How will life improve when you reach your goal?

_____

_____

_____

_____

_____

_____

_____

What can you see yourself doing when you reach your goal?

_____

_____

_____

_____

_____

_____

Describe a multisensory scene in which you obtain the benefits of reaching your goal. (Use present tense.)

_____

_____

_____

_____

_____

_____

_____

_____

_____

What behavioral suggestions can you give yourself to help you reach your goal?

_____

_____

_____

_____

_____

(The Wake-Up)

"I will awaken from hypnosis by counting to five. When I reach the number five, I will become fully alert and wide awake. One…beginning to awaken from hypnosis. Two…becoming aware of my surroundings…feeling satisfied, safe, and comfortable. Three…looking forward to positive results from this hypnosis session. Four…feeling absolutely wonderful. FIVE…FIVE…FIVE…now wide awake and fully alert."

Customized Suggestion Template

State your goal succinctly:

_____

_____

_____

_____

_____

_____

How will life improve when you reach your goal?

_____

_____

_____

_____

_____

_____

What can you see yourself doing when you reach your goal?

_____

_____

_____

_____

_____

_____

Describe a multisensory scene in which you obtain the benefits of reaching your goal. (Use present tense.)

_____

_____

_____

_____

_____

_____

_____

_____

_____

_____

What behavioral suggestions can you give yourself to help you reach your goal?

_____

_____

_____

_____

_____

_____

(The Wake-Up)

"I will awaken from hypnosis by counting to five. When I reach the number five, I will become fully alert and wide awake. One…beginning to awaken from hypnosis. Two…becoming aware of my surroundings…feeling satisfied, safe, and comfortable. Three…looking forward to positive results from this hypnosis session. Four…feeling absolutely wonderful. FIVE…FIVE…FIVE…now wide awake and fully alert."

Hypnosis Script

About the Author

Forbes Robbins Blair is the president of a personal-empowerment company called New Creations, which he began in 1990. He graduated from the University of Maryland and received his B.A. in Radio, TV, and Film. He became a professional hypnotherapist in 1997 after receiving certification in clinical hypnotherapy from the American Institute of Hypnotherapy in 1996. He began teaching the innovative principles of Instant Self-Hypnosis in a course called "How to Hypnotize Yourself with Your Eyes Open." Learned in knowledge of the subconscious mind, Forbes is also a dream consultant and facilitates dream groups and teaches classes on dream analysis, astral travel, and western mysticism. He has appeared on television and radio programs for his expertise in both hypnosis and dream analysis. He lives in Silver Spring, Maryland.